MW01505677

LOCKDOWN DRILLS

LOCKDOWN DRILLS

CONNECTING RESEARCH AND BEST PRACTICES FOR SCHOOL ADMINISTRATORS, TEACHERS, AND PARENTS

JACLYN SCHILDKRAUT AND
AMANDA B. NICKERSON

THE MIT PRESS   CAMBRIDGE, MASSACHUSETTS   LONDON, ENGLAND

© 2022 Massachusetts Institute of Technology

All rights reserved. No part of this book may be reproduced in any form by any electronic or mechanical means (including photocopying, recording, or information storage and retrieval) without permission in writing from the publisher.

The MIT Press would like to thank the anonymous peer reviewers who provided comments on drafts of this book. The generous work of academic experts is essential for establishing the authority and quality of our publications. We acknowledge with gratitude the contributions of these otherwise uncredited readers.

This book was set in ITC Stone Serif and Avenir LT Std by Westchester Publishing Services. Printed and bound in the United States of America.

Library of Congress Cataloging-in-Publication Data

Names: Schildkraut, Jaclyn, author. | Nickerson, Amanda B. (Amanda Beth), author.
Title: Lockdown drills : connecting research and best practices for school administrators, teachers, and parents / Jaclyn Schildkraut and Amanda B. Nickerson.
Description: Cambridge, Massachusetts : The MIT Press, [2022] | Includes bibliographical references and index. | Summary: "An examination of the role and impact of lockdown drills in America's schools, including consideration of arguments for and against these practices"—Provided by publisher.
Identifiers: LCCN 2021051252 | ISBN 9780262544160 (Paperback)
Subjects: LCSH: School crisis management—United States. | Emergency drills—United States. | School violence—Prevention—United States. | Schools—Safety measures—United States.
Classification: LCC LB2866.5 .S35 2022 | DDC 371.7/80973—dc23 /eng/20220423
LC record available at https://lccn.loc.gov/2021051252

10 9 8 7 6 5 4 3 2 1

To "Generation Columbine" . . .

To the students who have never known a world without lockdown or active shooter drills and who have been scared they might never see their families and friends again . . .

To the parents who have ever had to worry that their child was not coming home . . .

And to the educators tasked with keeping them safe.

CONTENTS

PREFACE

Although schools remain among the safest places for children, the need to prepare for a range of events, from the common to the statistically rare, that a building may face is undiminished. With respect to school lockdown drills, while some federal guidance is available, decisions as to how many of the drills should be conducted and the form they should take often fall to state or local policymakers, or both. Of course, there are other voices that should be part of the conversation about school safety—those of administrators, teachers, staff, parents, community stakeholders (including law enforcement and mental health professionals), and the students themselves. This book is designed to be a tool to help interested parties navigate the conversation about the role of lockdown drills as part of schools' emergency preparedness plans by bringing together the existing empirical research with the broader public and policy discussions about these practices.

In part I of the book, chapter 1 provides a basic background to how and why lockdown drills became a fixture in today's education landscape. In chapter 2, we consider the historical precedents that led to the introduction and subsequent expanded use of lockdown drills in schools. Chapter 3 addresses the current controversy surrounding lockdown drills that stems from the term being used to describe a variety of different practices, including options-based approaches specifically designed to respond to active shooters. Emergency preparedness practices may take a number of different forms, each with its own benefits and challenges. In chapter 4, we explore common arguments for and against lockdown drills to understand why these practices have become so divisive. Some knowledge of how these positions evolved can better inform efforts to move the national discussion forward.

Part II of the book examines existing and emerging scholarly research on the practice of lockdown drills. In chapter 5, we consider the different impacts that participating in lockdown drills have on students, the largest population in any school setting. Similarly, in chapter 6, we explore perceptions of these practices among the individuals who are charged with keeping students safe—schools' faculty, staff, and administration. Finally, in chapter 7, we move beyond the research on perceptions of these practices to try to discern whether participating in lockdown drills improves how accurately or effectively individuals respond to a potential threat.

Part III ties all these considerations together to understand the broader implications for policymakers who are implementing such practices. In chapter 8, we explore existing best practices issued by different organizations, including the National Association of School Psychologists and the National Association of School Resource Officers, that may help minimize the potential for trauma among participants when lockdown drills are implemented as part of an emergency preparedness plan. In chapter 9, we consider lockdown drills as one piece of a nearly $3 billion per year school safety and security industry, and what role these practices have in creating a layered approach to emergency preparedness, particularly in light of the US Department of Education's focal points for school safety.

Finally, in chapter 10, we consider the future of lockdown drills and other emergency preparedness practices. In this concluding chapter, we offer key takeaways to reflect on when thinking about lockdown drills moving forward, including how to increase buy-in, the importance of practice, and the role of drills in empowering students, faculty, and staff to stay safe. Though there is no one-size-fits-all solution to address the emergencies that our nation's schools face, these lessons can help students, educators, and policymakers work toward the goals of mitigating injuries and reducing loss of life in the gravest of emergencies.

As one reads through this book, it is important to keep in mind that drills, of which lockdowns are one type, are just one part of a complex school safety puzzle. Ensuring that schools are safe places for students and their educators requires a layered approach that begins long before a crisis happens with preventive measures and continues through the days, weeks, and years of recovery after one occurs. Comprehensive school safety plans should include measures related to prevention to avoid a crisis, such as having threat assessment teams in place. Protection involves taking action against potential threats (e.g., violence, disasters), such as by implementing physical security measures. Mitigation and response measures are designed to reduce the impact of the crisis, such as through the use of emergency protocols, and focus on saving lives, protecting property, reunifying students with their families, and meeting basic needs after an incident. Recovery emphasizes helping schools and communities rebuild and restore resources and services to affected individuals. Instituting appropriate policies and procedures for each phase of the crisis continuum will help schools ensure the most efficient response possible.

ACKNOWLEDGMENTS

Thank you to our research assistants, Hannah Grossman and Kirsten Klingaman, for their help with this project. Thank you to Tom Ristoff, Mike Thompson, and D.J. Brewster of Syracuse City School District (SCSD) for their support and continued partnership in conducting research related to the practices discussed. Thank you to the many research assistants from SUNY Oswego who assisted with data collection for our project, and to the administration, faculty, staff, students, and families of SCSD for their participation in several of the studies presented in this book. Finally, to our editor, Susan Buckley: thank you for believing in our vision and helping this book become a reality.

I

HOW DID WE GET HERE?

1

LOCKDOWN DRILLS AS A SCHOOL SAFETY PHENOMENON

Key Takeaways

- News headlines of "drills gone wrong" have led to calls to end these practices in schools.
- Among the concerns about drills is their potential impact on students' mental health and well-being.
- Lockdowns and active shooter drills are not the same thing, but they often are discussed as though they are.
- Responses to human-caused disasters such as an active shooting situation can draw inspiration from how we prepare for natural disasters.
- Practicing responding to human-caused disasters such as an active shooting situation is an important part of comprehensive school safety planning.

Each school day in America, it is likely that students in some part of the nation are participating in a lockdown drill. Although the requirements for these practices vary by state and sometimes even by school district within a state, the general steps often are the same. When the drill call is initiated, teachers lock their classroom doors, turn off the lights, and usher students out of sight of any interior windows (this area of the room is sometimes called a "hard corner"). Teachers and students remain silent as school safety teams and administrators check the building for compliance. Eventually the drill is released and the normal school day resumes.

For many, the thought of children and their educators practicing for a threat at school such as an active shooter is horrifying. It conjures up images of fearful children cowering in the corner, wondering whether they will ever go home again. It reminds us of educators at Sandy Hook Elementary School in Newtown, Connecticut, shielding their students with their bodies during the 2012 attack, making the ultimate sacrifice and giving their lives to protect others. It leads to imagining schools as war zones or fortresses. These thoughts are not entirely unfounded, a result of the images repeatedly featured in news coverage of high-profile school shootings. Few can forget the pictures and video clips of students with their hands in the air being led away from Columbine High School in Jefferson County, Colorado, by police, imagery that has been looped into news accounts of other attacks in the years since the 1999 events took place.

Not only are there differences between districts in the frequency with which these practices are conducted, there also are significant disparities in *how* they are carried out, with some schools going to extreme lengths to prepare students and teachers for emergencies. For instance, during one active shooter drill in Monticello, Indiana, teachers were shot with simunition, a type of nonlethal training ammunition, leaving them with physical injuries and emotional scars.[1] In Dayton, Ohio, students were exposed to the sound of simulated gunfire during drills.[2] Students also have been transformed into crisis actors, made up to look like shooting victims covered in fake blood or subjected to people (even including school administrators) dressed up as mock shooters and brandishing fake weapons to add a sense of realism to the drill.[3] Some schools have gone so far as to incorporate film footage taken during actual shootings into the drills to show students what they can expect in a real event.[4]

It is not surprising that stories of this sort make the headlines. Yet it is likely that they are the exception rather than the rule. If they were the latter, we would expect many more stories of "drills gone wrong," particularly since approximately 95 percent of public schools across the nation conduct lockdown drills each year.[5] This high prevalence of drills does not make these stories any less concerning, but it does highlight the need for a better understanding of the what, why, and how of lockdown drills.

END THE PRACTICE?

Stories about drills carried out in the manner just described have led to calls to end their use in schools, even though these practices have become increasingly more commonplace since Columbine. During the 2020 presidential campaign, for example, candidate Andrew Yang campaigned on a platform that included ending active shooter drills. In the same year, Everytown for Gun Safety, a prominent gun control organization started by former New York City mayor Michael Bloomberg, joined two of the nation's top teachers' unions—the National Education Association (NEA) and the American Federation of Teachers (AFT)—in publishing a white paper calling for an end to active shooter drills specifically (though lockdown drills often are incorrectly discussed interchangeably with active shooter drills).[6] At the core of these calls is the belief that participating in such drills is traumatizing students without making them safer. Parents across the nation share similar concerns. Proponents of ending active shooter drills suggest they lead to a range of negative outcomes, from anxiety, depression, and posttraumatic stress disorder (PTSD) to impaired academic performance and behavioral, emotional, and social problems.[7]

The concerns over the well-being of students are understandable in light of the prevalence of mental health–related diagnoses among children and adolescents. According to research compiled by the Centers for Disease Control and Prevention (CDC), among US youth ages three to seventeen, roughly 4.5 million, or 7.4 percent of this population, have been diagnosed with a behavioral problem.[8] Similarly, 4.4 million (7.1 percent) have been diagnosed with anxiety and 1.9 million (3.2 percent) with depression.[9] Additionally, these diagnoses are not made in isolation: approximately three out of every four children who have been diagnosed with depression also have a diagnosis of anxiety, and one-third of diagnoses of either anxiety or behavioral problems are accompanied by a diagnosis of depression.

Whether participating in lockdown or active shooter drills is contributing to these figures is unknown. Despite the widespread use of these practices in US primary and secondary schools, the research on their effects is alarmingly sparse. Although researchers have begun to collect the data and information necessary to better understand the impact of drills on those who participate in them, there is a long way to go. As such, much of the conversation about lockdown drills is rooted in emotion and anecdotes rather than evidence—but it is evidence that is needed to drive the policy decisions related to these practices. This book aims to be a cornerstone in building the foundation needed to help guide the conversation.

WHY DOES IT MATTER?

The stories we hear of students writing good-bye notes to their families, texting their parents begging for help, and even drafting wills indicating how they want their most treasured possessions divided if they do not come home are gut-wrenching. At the same time, these stories are born out of specific situations—actual lockdowns that are the result of a danger near or in the school for which action must be taken, or drills that are not called such. An investigation by the *Washington Post*, for example, found that on a typical day, more than six thousand real-world lockdowns occurred each day during the 2017–2018 school year, ultimately affecting over four million students—and that was just in the school districts located in the nation's thirty-one largest cities.[10] Additionally, in the more than twenty years since Columbine, over 187,000 students have been exposed to a shooting during their school day.[11] Although not every school shooting and threat that triggers a lockdown will rise to the level of a Columbine, they nevertheless highlight the need to be prepared in the event that the worst day happens.

These events are, however, quite rare, despite media portrayals that have fed public misperceptions about school shootings. In the context of crimes known to law enforcement, for example, homicide accounts for 0.1 percent of all offenses. Mass shootings represent a fraction of all homicides, with those incidents that take place at schools accounting for about one out of every four such attacks.[12] Youth homicides at schools are particularly rare, accounting for just 2 percent of all murders of individuals between the ages of five and eighteen (see figure 1.1, which contrasts the proportion

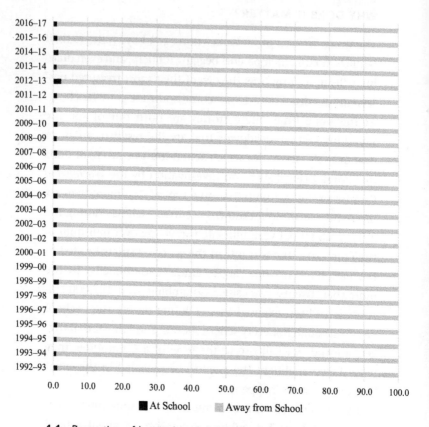

1.1 Proportion of homicides of children ages five to eighteen at and away from school. *Source:* Data from the School-Associated Violent Death Surveillance System (SAVD-SS).

of youth homicides occurring each academic year that happen at school versus away from schools).[13] The loss of one life at school, however, is one too many, and any steps that can be taken to save lives should be.

The rarity of homicide in schools highlights an important distinction that is often lost in the conversation about safety drills in schools—the difference between practices for active shooters and those for lockdowns. Active shooter drills, sometimes also called active attacker or active assailant drills, focus on a single type of event in which a person is engaged in trying to harm others inside the school building. Conversely, lockdown drills are used to prepare for *any* threat inside a building. While such threats may include those posed by active assailants, a lockdown drill can also be used to practice for situations involving an angry parent, a dangerous animal, or another internal threat that a school may be more likely to encounter. Recognizing and understanding this distinction can help people better understand the concerns surrounding these practices and the debate over whether or not they should be conducted.

THE PARKLAND EXAMPLE

One event in particular highlights what can happen when people lack preparation for the very worst day—the shooting at Marjory Stoneman Douglas High School in Parkland, Florida.[14] Prior to the February 14, 2018, shooting, the school did not have an established active attacker or lockdown policy. Teachers had received little training in how to respond to an active attacker at the school. Students had received no instruction in this area, and no drills had been conducted at the school in the year prior that would have allowed faculty, staff, students, and administrators to practice their responses and build up the necessary muscle memory—a term used to describe the body's ability to engage in specific actions it has been trained in even when cognitive processing is impaired by stress or other factors.[15]

When the shooting erupted in one of the school's buildings just after 2:21 p.m. local time, many occupants did not know how to respond. On the first floor, where eleven individuals were killed, many did not have time to respond as the shooting unfolded very quickly; others were hindered by furniture that prevented them from taking cover in the rooms' "hard corners." Hard corners provide protection because they allow individuals to be out of the line of sight from a threat inside the building. Figure 1.2 illustrates where a hard corner may be located in a classroom setting. These corners typically are located farthest from the door into the classroom and along the same wall, which reduces the angle of vision from the hallway window.

The building's fire alarm was activated almost immediately, triggered by dust falling as a result of the reverberations of the gun shooting. As teachers and students sought shelter on the second floor (no one was injured or killed on that level), students on the third floor had begun evacuating in a manner consistent with a fire drill. Although they had heard the faint sounds of gunfire, they could not fully make out the noises and therefore responded to the alarm as they had been trained to. By the time they realized what was going on mid-evacuation, it was too late for some. When the perpetrator made his way up to the third floor, he opened fire, killing

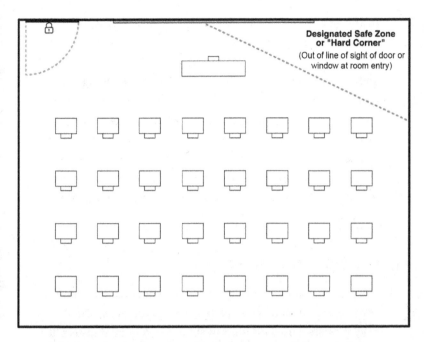

1.2 Example of a classroom with the hard corner designated. *Source:* Authors' rendering; lock icon licensed under Creative Commons (Attribution 3.0 Unported).

six of the seventeen people murdered that day and injuring four others before dropping the gun and fleeing the school.

Would being trained in how to respond to an active shooter before the attack took place have changed the outcome? Possibly, particularly for the victims on the third floor, but we will never know for certain. The lack of training and practice also was not the only failure that day. There were other issues related to the failure to call a Code Red (the school's designation for an immediate threat, which was further compounded by the lack of a formal policy concerning how and when such a call should be made), classroom doors that could be locked only from the exterior (in the hallway), the lack of public address speakers in the hallways to alert the building occupants to what was taking place, and more. Events like the Parkland shooting, much like their responses, represent perfect storms, an alignment of numerous discrete factors that results in a horrific outcome. That is why it is important for schools to take an all-hazards approach to safety and emergency preparedness, of which lockdowns are one important component.

KEEPING IT IN CONTEXT

One way to approach thinking about lockdown drills as a necessary component of a comprehensive school safety plan is to view human-caused disasters as similar to natural disasters. It is hard to imagine schools in the Midwest, for example, without a plan for tornadoes, just as it is hard to imagine schools along the West Coast not being prepared for earthquakes. These events are unpredictable and can happen with little to no warning, so over the years, schools and communities have established and implemented plans to keep themselves safe. They practice these plans to make sure everyone knows how to respond before the emergency happens, and then they adhere to the protocol if it does.

Responses to human-caused disasters require the same commitment to preparation because they are often similarly unpredictable. Much as natural disasters require communities worldwide to adapt to new and emerging threats resulting from climate change, responses to human-caused disasters also need to be flexible. Although today in US schools it seems almost impossible to imagine a world without active shooter or lockdown drills, such practices were not common for students who attended K–12 schools before Columbine. Students in the 1960s, for example, faced a different threat as America found itself embroiled in the Cold War and preparing for the possibility of a Soviet nuclear attack. Similarly, future generations likely will face entirely different threats for which emergency response plans have yet to be designed.

2

WHY LOCKDOWN DRILLS?
A LOOK AT HOW WE GOT HERE

Key Takeaways

- School safety drills have been commonplace since the 1950s, although they were used sporadically prior to that time.
- The earliest drills were intended to protect students and staff at schools from nuclear attacks (duck-and-cover drills).
- Today, drills are part of emergency preparedness for fires, tornadoes, earthquakes, and more.
- Lockdown drills specifically became common practice after the 1999 shooting at Columbine High School.
- Door locks (an essential component of lockdown drills) have been found to be the most successful lifesaving device in an active shooter situation.

Each day, students in different parts of the nation participate in lockdown drills, a practice that is followed in 95 percent of US schools.[1] This estimate does not take into account the proportion of students who take part in actual lockdowns, either because of a credible threat or because of a false alarm. An study by the *Washington Post* estimated that in the 2017–2018 school year, more than four million students were exposed to at least one real lockdown.[2] The paper's analysis, however, tallied only lockdowns reported in schools and districts in the nation's thirty-one largest cities, so the true breadth of how many students experience an actual lockdown annually remains unknown.

In the context of school safety and preparedness, lockdowns and their associated drills are relatively new, emerging as a widespread practice only after the 1999 shooting at Columbine High School in Jefferson County, Colorado. Yet the use of school emergency preparedness drills dates back to the Cold War era, when duck-and-cover drills were practiced in anticipation of possible nuclear attacks from the Soviet Union. Since then, other forms of safety drills have been introduced in schools to prepare students, faculty, staff, and administrators for both natural and human-caused disasters. In this chapter, we look at the historical precedents for lockdown drills, including duck-and-cover drills, and practices to prepare for fires and such natural disasters as tornadoes and earthquakes. We also explore how lockdown drills have evolved since their introduction after Columbine.

DUCK-AND-COVER DRILLS

With the end of World War II, the United States transitioned into a different conflict, this time with the Soviet Union, as previous tensions over differences in geopolitical and economic ideologies resurfaced. The period of heightened threat that came to be known as the Cold War emerged after President Harry S. Truman introduced the Truman Doctrine on March 12, 1947, which pledged support from the United States to countries, including Greece and Turkey, threatened by Soviet communism. The doctrine became the cornerstone of America's foreign policy at the time and eventually led to the creation of the North Atlantic Treaty Organization, or NATO.[3]

Emerging from World War II, the United States was considered to have a monopoly on nuclear weapons such as those used to bomb the Japanese cities of Hiroshima and Nagasaki in 1945. In August 1949, however, the Soviet Union tested its own version of the bomb used in the attack on Nagasaki, known as the RDS-1, and production of additional units began soon after.[4] This led to growing concern over the threat of nuclear attacks on US soil and the need to prepare schools to respond if they happened. Out of this fear, duck-and-cover drills were born.

The first surprise cover drills were held in public, private, and parochial schools in target cities—New York City, Philadelphia, Detroit, Chicago, Milwaukee, Fort Worth, Los Angeles, and San Francisco—beginning in August 1950 and running through April 1951.[5] To ensure that students were prepared to respond at any given moment, teachers would yell "Drop!" without warning. Students then had to kneel down, typically sheltering under their desks, and cover their heads and necks with their arms while teachers checked to ensure they were performing the steps correctly. Drills varied in frequency, at first weekly, then shifting to biweekly and soon monthly as schools tried to figure out the best way to promote civilian defense.

While decisions about drill practices initially were left up to the schools and districts, President Truman soon provided additional guidance with the introduction of the Federal Civil Defense Administration (FCDA) in January 1951. Although implementation and funding of practices remained states' responsibilities after the creation of the FCDA, the agency was tasked with creating educational materials that could be used as part of such efforts. The FCDA introduced Bert the Turtle in 1951 in a comic book designed to teach children how to respond during a nuclear attack by showing that it was no different from how they should respond to any form of everyday danger. Bert appeared in a short film, made in a collaboration between the FCDA and the US Office of Civil Defense, titled *Duck and Cover*.[6] The film blended animations of Bert with real students in classrooms demonstrating what to do in case of a nuclear attack. All materials provided were free of any frightening elements, instead relying on cheerfulness to educate, in an attempt to minimize the traumatic impact on children participating in the drills. A letter sent to Brooklyn,

2.1 A page from the FCDA's *Duck and Cover* pamphlet produced in 1951.

New York, parents from the Board of Education noted that teachers were instructed to smile during drills and to treat the practice as a game to assuage student anxiety.

In the early 1960s, the heightened concern over possible atomic bomb attacks began to wane. The Cuban missile crisis had been averted, and President John F. Kennedy entered the United States into a test-ban treaty with Russia, easing tensions between the two superpowers. Thereafter, duck-and-cover practices seemingly were no longer needed and quickly were phased out of schools' emergency preparedness plans. Other concerns subsequently required schools to adapt their thinking and their practices to protect students and educators from new and emerging threats.

FIRE DRILLS

While schools across the nation focused on conducting duck-and-cover drills in the 1950s, one incident highlighted the need for a different form of emergency preparedness practice: fire drills. On December 1, 1958, a fire broke out in the basement of Our Lady of the Angels Roman Catholic Church's grade school in Chicago after students were instructed by their teacher to dispose of some waste in the boiler room.[7] By the time the students made it back to the classroom, there were reports of smoke being smelled. Recognizing that there was a problem, teachers began trying to evacuate their students from the building, though they lacked any specific protocol to guide them in the process.

Chaos and pandemonium ensued. As teachers insisted everyone get out of the building, scared students on the second floor of the school refused to leave. When they would not crawl down the stairs as directed, they were pushed. Others remained in their classrooms, trying to prevent smoke from entering the room by covering cracks with desks and books. Some even stayed in their seats and prayed for help. As the fire quickly spread through the building, which was constructed of combustible material inside a brick shell and lacked any sprinkler system, windows were shattered, creating avenues for some students to escape by shimmying down pipes or jumping from the building, landing either on adjacent roofs or on the ground. The broken windows also enabled an endless flow of oxygen that fed the fire, causing it to spread more quickly. By the time the blaze was under control, ninety-two children and three nuns had been killed.

Prior to the tragedy at Our Lady of the Angels, fire safety practices had started to appear in schools as a result of other particularly lethal events, including the March 4, 1908, fire at Lake View School in Collinwood, Ohio, that killed 172 students, two teachers, and a rescuer, and the May 17, 1923, blaze at the Cleveland School in Camden, South Carolina, that left seventy-seven adults and children dead.[8] In fact, Chicago schools had been conducting fire drills prior to the Our Lady of the Angels tragedy, and operational guidance for how such practices were to be carried out was provided after an inquest spearheaded by the mayor's office in 1925 revealed that just 15 percent of schools were doing them correctly.[9] Within six months after uniform drill guidance was provided, the efficiency rate had improved to 100 percent. It is unclear, however, whether the church school specifically had participated in such practices prior to the fire.

After the Chicago tragedy, changes were enacted nationwide to address not only building construction and design flaws that nurtured fires rather than preventing their spread but also how building occupants were taught to respond in case a fire broke out. Fire drills are designed to teach individuals how to evacuate a building quickly and safely if needed. Elements of a fire drill include instilling awareness not only of a person's primary evacuation route and exit based on location within the building at the time of the fire or other emergency but also of back-up exits in case the primary evacuation route cannot be accessed. Fire drills also allow schools to test their capacity to quickly and safely evacuate buildings and to remind building occupants of their assembly points. Although such drills were conducted as early as the 1800s,[10] their use was expanded considerably after the 1958 fire in Chicago.

With no federal regulations regarding the number of fire drills that schools are required to conduct annually and the US Department of Education providing only limited guidance about fire safety,[11] decisions about the conduct of such practices typically fall to the states. Some states, including New Jersey and Alabama, require schools to conduct fire drills once a month. Others, including New York and Oklahoma, set a specific number of practices that must be conducted annually but leave it up to the districts or the schools to decide when the drills take place. Some states, such as Virginia, further mandate that a greater number of drills must occur at the beginning of the school year to serve as a refresher for returning students and as practice for new students to learn the procedures. Taken together, all but one state, Missouri, have mandated guidelines in place for fire drills.

Since the Chicago tragedy in 1958, no other school fire has claimed the lives of more than ten people.[12] A 2020 analysis by the National Fire Protection Association reported that, on average nationally, one person dies in a school fire each year.[13] Fires in schools also account for just 1 percent of all structural fires in the United States in a given year. Yet despite their rarity, schools continue to conduct fire drills, ensuring they are prepared to respond if they are ever faced with such a situation.

DRILLS FOR NATURAL DISASTERS

In addition to fire drills, schools also prepare for a range of natural disasters, including tornadoes and earthquakes. According to the National Center for Education Statistics, in the 2017–2018 school year, 94 percent of US public schools had a written emergency response plan with specific procedures for responding to natural disasters and 83 percent conducted the shelter-in-place drills that are used in such situations.[14] The broader term "shelter in place" is most commonly used for responses to hazards outside the school for which individuals are brought inside to separate themselves from the threat, but sheltering in place also may be used to protect against dangers inside the building, such as a hazmat situation.[15] The types of natural disasters that a school or district has plans in place for, however, will be context-specific, as not all communities are vulnerable to the same types of threat.[16] States in the Midwest and South, for example, are more likely to practice tornado drills, while schools in the West may focus preparedness efforts on earthquakes or even tsunamis.

Tornado and earthquake drills are said to have evolved out of the civil defense (duck-and-cover) drills of the 1950s and 1960s. Indeed, the actions taken during one of these practices or real-world exercises largely mirror their predecessor:

students and educators drop, get themselves in a secure space (for earthquakes, this may be a doorway or under sturdy furniture; for tornadoes, it is often in an interior room or corridor that is structurally stable and away from windows), and cover their heads to protect against falling debris. Schools vulnerable to tornadoes also may have storm shelters on the property, either within the building (e.g., the basement) or close by so that individuals can get to them quickly if a storm is approaching, and practicing evacuating to such locations may be part of the drill.

Although there are no specific mandates for drills related to natural disasters at the federal level, the US Department of Education provides resources for schools related to responding to such emergencies and restoring the educational environment if one occurs.[17] Other federal agencies, including the National Severe Storms Laboratory (part of the National Oceanic and Atmospheric Administration, or NOAA), the National Weather Service, and the Federal Emergency Management Agency (FEMA), provide guidance on severe weather preparation or provide resources to help educate students about these hazards.[18] Still, just as with fire drills, requirements for schools as to the number of practices for natural disasters and when they should be conducted typically are left up to the state, leading to variability nationwide. Notably, although severe weather is considerably more common than school fires, drills for severe weather typically are conducted less often than fire drills.

LOCKDOWN DRILLS

When more than 1,900 students, along with faculty, staff, and administrators, entered Columbine High School in Jefferson

County, Colorado, on April 20, 1999, they had no idea what that day would bring.[19] At around 11:20 a.m., the school became the scene of the most well-known mass shooting in US history when two seniors opened fire after a failed bombing attempt. While some students and teachers were able to flee the school to safety, hundreds were locked down in classrooms and offices for the duration of the nearly fifty-minute rampage, plus the time it took law enforcement to clear the building and evacuate survivors. Although the perpetrators had four guns and nearly one hundred improvised explosive devices such as pipe bombs and Molotov cocktails, they never once tried to breach a locked door. Instead, the thirteen individuals killed and the two dozen injured that day were all in open spaces—outside the building on school grounds, in a hallway—or in an unlocked area, the library.

Like most schools at the time, Columbine did not have a plan in place for responding to active shooters. Despite a number of school shootings earlier in the 1990s, such events were still viewed as isolated incidents. The Columbine shooting changed that perception. Replacing the view that gun violence was an inner-city problem, Columbine highlighted that no community was immune to such threats. In its aftermath, schools and districts nationwide scrambled to implement practices to protect students if a Columbine-style attack were to happen in their community.

One of the recommendations offered in the Columbine Review Commission's report was that schools conduct annual crisis drills; the report noted that "school-based training and preparedness rehearsals are critical components of an effective emergency plan."[20] While the school had plans in place prior to April 20 to address such common emergencies as fires, these protocols were insufficient to handle a disaster of Columbine's magnitude. Even without formalized lockdown procedures in place on the day of the shooting, however, the commission noted that engaging in the steps of the practice—locking doors, turning off lights, moving out of sight of any corridor windows—likely saved countless lives that day, particularly as the library, where the majority of fatalities and injuries occurred, could not be secured.

Where the term "lockdown" as used in relation to schools (compared to its use in the stay-at-home orders issued during the COVID-19 pandemic or to secure a prison during a security breach) originated remains somewhat unknown. It has been suggested that the term was first used in schools in Southern California in the late 1970s as a response to drive-by shootings and other street crimes that were occurring near school buildings. Also known as "drive-by drills," "drop drills," "crisis drills," or "bullet drills," these practices were similar to the previous decade's duck-and-cover drills: when the teachers yelled "Drop!," students got under their desks or lay flat on the floor and covered their heads.

Although the *Report on Indicators of School Crime and Safety* (ISCS), published annually by the National Center for Education Statistics (NCES), an agency of the US Department of Education, historically has included data on school-based practices related to safety and discipline, such as the use of metal detectors, video surveillance, and drug sweeps, it was not until the 2015–2016 school year that the NCES began tracking and reporting on the use of lockdown drills.[21] That year, it was reported that 95 percent of public schools were drilling students in active shooter emergency procedures, a figure that has remained steady. Similarly, in the 2015–2016 academic year, 92 percent of schools reported having written procedures to respond to active shooter events, a steady increase from the 2003–2004 academic year, when 78.5 percent of schools had such plans.

Despite the proliferation of both written plans and drills, however, there is no consistency in either as a result of the absence of a national standard for responding to an active shooter situation.[22] This raised the question as to what protocol schools were using to prepare. In the years following Columbine, several options emerged. The first was the A.L.I.C.E. program, introduced in 2000 by a small private security company based in the Dallas–Fort Worth area of Texas.[23] The options-based approach of A.L.I.C.E. was designed to provide schools with different choices, including and beyond the traditional lockdown: "Alert" others of the danger and initiate the lockdown; "Lockdown" using the typical procedures; "Inform" authorities about any details of the unfolding situation (e.g., how many people are in each room, where the shooter is located); "Counter" if confronted by the assailant; and "Evacuate" the building if able.

The protocol Avoid Deny Defend was introduced in 2004 by the Advanced Law Enforcement Rapid Response Training (ALERRT) Center in San Marcos, Texas.[24] This protocol advocates putting as much distance as possible between an individual and a threat (Avoid), creating barriers to prevent the threat from reaching you when getting away is not possible (Deny), and fighting back as a last resort when the remaining options are not available (Defend). Elements of situational awareness, such as paying attention to one's surroundings and having an exit strategy, also are key aspects of the protocol. A follow-up program, Civilian Response to Active Shooter Events (CRASE), also is offered by ALERRT.

Following the September 27, 2006, shooting at Platte Canyon High School in Bailey, Colorado, the Standard Response Protocol (SRP) was introduced by the "I Love U Guys" Foundation, created by the parents of Emily Keyes, who was killed in the attack.[25] Unlike A.L.I.C.E. and Avoid Deny Defend, which focus solely on responding to armed assailants, SRP is an all-hazards plan for schools to respond to emergencies; it includes lockdowns. In addition to plans for lockdowns (used when threats are inside the building), SRP also offers operational guidance for lockout / secure (when threats are on or near school grounds), evacuation (e.g., fire drill), shelter-in-place (used for weather related emergencies), and hold-in-place (to keep hallways clear in instances of medical emergencies and the like) procedures. Additionally, SRP uses language from the National Incident Management System (NIMS), part of FEMA, to help improve communication between first responders and civilians during a crisis.

The most well-known response strategy is Run Hide Fight, which was developed for first responders through a collaboration between the City of Houston and the Department of Homeland Security in response to the 2008 terrorist attacks in Mumbai, India.[26] The earliest version of this guidance advised individuals facing an active shooter situation to "evacuate" their location if safe to do so, "hide out" if evacuation was not possible, and "take action" if confronted by the shooter and in imminent danger. In mid-2012, just days prior to the July

20 shooting at an Aurora, Colorado, movie theater, Houston released a training video and accompanying materials from the initiative with the more common messaging of Run Hide Fight, and in 2013, the US Department of Education adopted the strategy as a recommendation for schools.[27]

Although these various options are available for use, as are others that have drawn inspiration from them, no data exist as to how common any given program is in schools across the nation. Similarly, as with other types of drills discussed in this chapter, there are no federal mandates for what such practices should look like or how often preparedness drills should be conducted. Decisions consequently are left up to the states, leading to considerable variability not only in type and frequency but in whether such practices are required in the first place. The appendix provides an overview of active shooter and lockdown drill requirements by state.

WHY LOCKDOWNS SPECIFICALLY?

At nearly fifty minutes, the Columbine shooting was an anomaly—in reality, the majority of mass and school shootings are over in five minutes or less.[28] Consequently, the goal of the lockdown is to create distance between the assailant and the intended targets, which is achieved by the main word of the protocol, "lock." After the 2012 attack at Sandy Hook Elementary School in Newtown, Connecticut, the advisory commission charged with reviewing the incident and response highlighted the importance of door locks in saving lives during active shooting events.[29] The very first recommendation in the report was that all classrooms should be fitted with doors that could be locked from the interior, which would prevent teachers from having to go into the hall to secure the room and risk encountering the assailant, as was the case on the day of the shooting.

This recommendation stems from the fact that in all of the mass shootings that have occurred in schools, no one has been killed in a locked room because the door lock failed. There were three instances, however, of people being killed in rooms with locked doors. The first was during the March 21, 2005, shooting at Red Lake High School in Red Lake, Minnesota, in which the perpetrator shot through the window of a classroom to gain access.[30] Even with shooting at the locks, he had been unsuccessful in gaining entry; instead, the lock had melted. In the 2006 shooting at Platte Canyon High School, the perpetrator who killed Emily Keyes was barricaded in the classroom—behind the locked door—with her.[31] When the SWAT team breached the room with explosives, the perpetrator shot Emily before being killed by responding officers. More recently, though the perpetrator of the February 14, 2018, shooting at Marjory Stoneman Douglas High School in Parkland, Florida, killed a number of students who were in classrooms with locked doors on the building's first floor, he never gained access to a single room.[32] In each of these instances, the door locks themselves did not fail.

In addition to the Sandy Hook Advisory Commission, other organizations, including the School Infrastructure Safety Council and the National School Shield Task Force, have echoed the need for door locks that can be secured from the interior, preferably in a manner that does not require fine motor skills, which may be compromised as a result of stress; an example is

deadbolts that do not need a key.[33] By instructing students and
their educators to secure behind locked doors, lockdown guidance not only creates physical distance between the shooter
and the intended victims but also adds more time on the clock
as the perpetrator is unlikely to be able to breach the door
before law enforcement arrives on scene. It bears noting that
lockdowns may not be possible when a shooting begins in a
common area such as a cafeteria or gym. In such situations, the
lockdown protocol is augmented with other strategies, such as
evacuating the building.

UNDERSTANDING DRILLS AS PART OF DISASTER EDUCATION

Disaster education is a pedagogical approach used both in
and out of schools to prepare individuals for emergency
situations they may encounter.[34] Such education serves to
"build a culture of safety and resilience," in the words of
a United Nations report.[35] Disaster education entails teaching individuals about the risks related to different types of
disasters that could have an impact on perceptions or beliefs
about such threats, and ways to mitigate the danger, including potential injuries and damages, through preparedness
efforts.[36] A secondary objective of disaster education is to
encourage individuals to take a proactive approach to prevention and harm mitigation through fostering behavioral
changes.

   While different methods are used to deliver disaster education, preparedness drills like those discussed here fall under
the rubric of *performance pedagogy*, which involves rehears-
ing response strategies for a particular hazard or emergency.

There are two overarching goals of such practices. The first is to familiarize individuals with a specific set of actions to take when responding to a given emergency. The second goal is to build muscle memory,[37] so that these actions become second nature and can be executed when the individual encounters some type of cognitive roadblock, such as stress or fear. In other words, in situations where individuals are exposed to stressors, either external (e.g., seeing a shooter with a gun) or internal (e.g., fear from seeing or hearing a firearm), that limit their cognitive functioning, they still can respond physically as they were trained to, with less mental effort required. This can potentially reduce vulnerability to victimization during the disaster. Drills also provide participants with an opportunity to reflect on what has taken place and identify areas for improvement, which can help improve the procedural integrity of the practice over time.[38]

Incorporating disaster education into the school environment is critical because students, teachers, administrators, and staff are vulnerable to crises that unfold in or around their building. Incorporating emergency preparedness into the school experience has several benefits. First, students receive a formal education about different types of hazards, including their causes, which can help promote an accurate understanding of the dangers and their associated risks.[39] Second, this education has been found not only to increase knowledge of and awareness about disaster risks but also to improve attitudes toward related preparedness efforts, such as drills. Disaster education also has been found to reduce fear over these hazards and potential victimization from them.[40] Finally, providing disaster education helps disseminate knowledge related to hazards, their risks, and appropriate responses to them more broadly as students take this information home and share it with their families.

Preparing students to respond if they find themselves in an active shooter situation may seem alarming, yet the Columbine, Sandy Hook, and Parkland tragedies underscore the need not only to have such protocols in place but to also make sure they are known and can be employed efficiently if needed. The lack of an agreed-upon standard for these drills has led to considerable variation, including practices that make headlines for all the wrong reasons. The result has been a widespread outcry over lockdown and active shooter drills, even though they are not the same. The next chapter delves further into the differences between drills and exercises, both broadly and in relation to lockdowns specifically, and considers the utility of each in the context of school emergency preparedness.

3

WHAT ARE LOCKDOWN DRILLS?
DIFFERENTIATING DRILLS AND EXERCISES

Key Takeaways

- Exercises are used to develop, test, or validate emergency response plans and capabilities.
- A drill is a type of exercise designed to test a single operation. It provides an opportunity for participants to practice or maintain skills.
- Commonly practiced drills in schools include lockdown, lockout, evacuate (e.g., fire drills), shelter-in-place, and hold (or hold-in-place) drills.
- Lockdown drills, in contrast to options-based approaches, involve practicing a specific procedure that can be used for any threat inside a school building.
- Decisions about exercises and drills should be made by multidisciplinary school safety teams.

In preparation for crisis situations, schools have emergency operations plans that detail how to respond to a variety of threats and hazards, including but not limited to natural disasters (e.g., hurricanes, earthquakes, floods), accidental death or injury, kidnapping, bomb threats, hazardous chemical releases, acts of violence and terrorism, and suicide. To test how these procedures may work under various conditions, it is important to practice different parts of each plan. Doing so is a standard across various industries, such as manufacturing, medicine, and technology: once a safety plan is devised, it must be tested under different conditions to ensure that it is adequate to its goal, and schools are no exception. Perhaps one of the most popular and well-rehearsed ways in which schools test plans is the fire drill. In devising an appropriate fire drill, schools collaborate with the local fire department to ensure that students, faculty, staff, and visitors know how to properly evacuate the building. To illustrate how such a collaboration may be helpful, let's consider a hypothetical situation in which a school adds a roundabout at the front entrance to improve traffic flow and then conducts a drill. During the drill, it becomes apparent that the fire truck is now unable to access the hydrant. Had this blockage occurred during an actual fire, it could have resulted in injury, property destruction, and even death. Running a drill allows a school to identify a gap and revise the plan and procedure to make it more workable before an emergency happens.

To better understand lockdown drills, it is helpful to understand the bigger picture of drills and exercises in school safety planning. Part of the controversy over and confusion about lockdowns stems from the incorrect use of terms interchangeably for different drills and exercises. In this chapter, we describe the differences among these various practices and the role each plays in fostering a culture of preparedness. We also discuss options-based approaches, which are used specifically for active shooter and armed assailant scenarios, and how these and more involved exercises differ from lockdown drills. We conclude the chapter by explaining how drills and exercises can be used in conjunction with one another (with the appropriate planning and resources) to help schools prepare for emergencies that may occur.

WHAT ARE EXERCISES?

Exercises are events or activities designed to develop, test, or validate emergency response plans, procedures, and capabilities.[1] In the context of school safety planning, exercises provide opportunities to practice the plan, often with community agencies—the fire department, police department, or other emergency responders—and to identify any issues that need to be remedied.[2] Delivery options can vary from discussion-based practices to operations-based exercises, which are more action-oriented. Discussion-based exercises familiarize participants with the emergency response plans and procedures. They may include seminars, which are lectures with groups to provide a common understanding, or workshops, which involve more interaction and focus on developing specific plans, procedures, or agreements related to the emergency response.

To further improve the understanding of roles and procedures during emergencies and identify the strengths and weaknesses of plans, tabletop exercises are recommended by the US Department of Homeland Security (DHS). A tabletop exercise involves small-group discussion about the actions to take in response to a hypothetical emergency scenario. For example, a school's multidisciplinary safety team may meet quarterly to run through tabletop exercises with different scenarios (a chemical spill, a bomb threat, a bus accident) to ensure that each team member knows what to do and how to work together in these situations. The final discussion-based exercise identified is a game. This is a structured form of play with clear rules and procedures during which individuals or teams make decisions about actions to take in response to hypothetical crisis scenarios, and explore the consequences of the decisions made.

In contrast to discussion-based exercises, operations-based exercises involve real-time responses and may entail the use of communication systems or activation of personnel or resources; they include drills, functional exercises, and full-scale exercises. In a functional exercise, multiple agencies use the incident command system (ICS) to implement the emergency response plan and procedures with participants reacting to a simulated threat such as an armed intruder or a hostage situation. This type of exercise is used to evaluate response capabilities in a realistic environment. Therefore, it may involve the use of actors to perform the roles of perpetrators or victims or the use of props such as nonlethal weapons to simulate more realistic scenarios. A full-scale exercise deploys all resources, including public information services, communications systems, response equipment, and personnel, coordinated across multiple agencies and jurisdictions to implement and analyze plans and procedures that have previously been developed through discussion-based exercises and practiced during less involved operations-based exercises. Full-scale exercises involve establishing an emergency operations center (also known as the command post, or the coordination hub for decision-makers and first responders to gather information, coordinate, and manage the response in a crisis) and activating the ICS.

WHAT ARE DRILLS?

Drills are one form of an operations-based exercise that allows stakeholders, including school personnel and community partners such as first responders and local emergency management staff, to become familiar with procedures to be carried out in an emergency by practicing responding to a scenario using the actual school grounds and buildings.[3] Typically, drills are undertaken to test a single operation, such as a lockdown or an evacuation protocol. They also provide training for participants to practice or maintain skills. Whereas exercises are used primarily to test capacity, drills are designed to assess memory.[4]

Since drills are used to teach and practice skills for a particular operation or situation, schools are encouraged to use many different types. Although the number and type of drills that schools conduct vary by state, table 3.1 includes the most commonly practiced procedures in schools, their associated steps, and the threats or hazards to which they apply, listed from most to least severe. Although these drills prepare staff and students in the necessary actions to take for a specific emergency response procedure, they also may be applied to other threats or hazards as the situation warrants. For example, if there is a chemical spill, the school may evacuate occupants if there is an immediate threat of harm (e.g., should the spillage contains combustible material) or issue a shelter-in-place order, depending on the location and other safety issues (whether the spill can be quickly contained and neutralized).

What is most important is that the response strategies are clear to staff and students so that they can follow the

Table 3.1 School crisis drills: Type, typical procedure, and applicable threat/Hazard

Type	Typical Procedure	Applicable Threat/ Hazard
Lockdown	• If possible, gather students from hallways and common areas nearby into classroom. • Lock the door. • Turn off lights (note: this varies by jurisdiction). • Move to area of classroom out of sight of door or hallway. • Maintain silence. • Take attendance. • Do not respond or communicate (by phone, or to an announcement, fire alarm, or door knock). • Remain in place until released by law enforcement.	Used for incidents that pose an immediate threat of violence in the school (e.g., an armed assailant, a dangerous animal, an act of violence in school).
Secure (also called lockout or reverse evacuation)	• Enter or remain inside a secured school building. • Lock all outside doors and windows. • Take attendance. • Do not allow visitors, students, or staff to enter or leave the building after it is secured.	Used for incidents that pose an immediate risk outside the school (e.g., a fugitive from law).
Evacuate	• Exit the classroom and close the door. • Use a pre-identified route (or secondary route, if needed) to lead students to a designated assembly area. • Take attendance.	Used when there is a hazard inside the building and it is safer to evacuate than to remain in the building (e.g., a fire, an indoor chemical spill, a bomb threat).

Type	Typical Procedure	Applicable Threat/ Hazard
Hold (or hold in place)	• Remain in assigned classroom. • For students and staff in hallways, return to assigned classroom if possible. • Take attendance.	Used in short-term emergencies to limit the movement of staff and students (e.g., a medical emergency).
Shelter in place	• Move to a predetermined safe area (e.g., lowest floor level; interior room or hallway away from exterior doors and windows). • Close doors and windows. • Turn off fans and classroom ventilation (designated staff turn off main shut-off valves for HVAC). • Use barrier materials (e.g., duct tape, plastic sheeting) to seal gaps in windows and doors if instructed to do so.	Used for severe weather or hazardous materials release when it is safer to secure or shelter in the building.

Source: Stephen E. Brock, Amanda B. Nickerson, Melissa A. Reeves, et al., *School Crisis Prevention and Intervention: The PREPaRE Model*, 2nd ed. (Bethesda, MD: National Association of School Psychologists, 2016); "I Love U Guys" Foundation, "The Standard Response Protocol K–12" (2021); Safe Schools New York, *Emergency Response* (2015); Texas School Safety Center, *Drill Guidance* (n.d.); US Department of Education, Office of Elementary and Secondary Education, Office of Safe and Healthy Students, "Guide for Developing High-Quality School Emergency Operations Plans" (2013).

procedures safely and efficiently, with the recognition that circumstances dictate which protocol to follow. As stated by Deputy Chief A. J. DeAndrea of the Arvada, Colorado, Police Department, "Tactics are intel driven, but the environment dictates tactics." Stated in other words by John-Michael Keyes of the "I Love U Guys" Foundation, "What we plan is based on what we know, but what we do is based on where we are."[5] Staff and students should be fully prepared to follow the protocols, but there also is a need to be flexible about which procedure is utilized, based on the situation. For example, although lockdowns typically are the best protocol to follow when there is an armed assailant in a building, if people are in an open area where they cannot secure themselves behind a locked door, they should know that they have the option to evacuate to safety.

There is wide variability in mandates and practices regarding drills. Several states require that safety drills (which include lockdowns) be conducted monthly, with most alternating fire or evacuation practices with other drills. For example, Utah specifies that the school must conduct one emergency drill each month, alternating fire drills with other practices such as shelter-in-place, earthquake, lockdown, lockout, or a bomb threat response drill. Similarly, Washington state mandates that schools conduct one safety drill per month, including shelter-in-place, lockdown, and evacuation drills. Washington is one of the few states that explicitly encourages schools to work with local law enforcement to conduct their practices, recommending one tabletop exercise, one functional exercise, and two full-scale exercises in a four-year period. Other states are explicit about the types of drills and corresponding frequencies. For example, Texas requires schools to conduct the following drills annually: four fire drills (two per semester), two lockdown drills (one per semester), one evacuation drill, and two shelter-in-place drills (one for hazardous materials and one for severe weather). Similarly, New York requires eight evacuation drills (for fire) and four lockdown drills each year.

Some states mandate a specific drill around an active shooter or armed intruder/assailant. For example, Tennessee mandates one armed intruder drill be conducted annually and in coordination with local law enforcement, while South Carolina requires at least two active shooter/intruder drills. Missouri mandates that all school personnel participate in annual training and a simulated armed intruder response drill led by law enforcement using the state's Active Shooter and Intruder Response Training (ASIRT) model. Conversely, some states require only one drill or exercise per year and allow flexibility as to what is included. For example, North Carolina requires each school to hold a full schoolwide table-top exercise and drill based that includes a practice school lockdown, and Colorado mandates an all-hazards drill but does not specify further other than saying it can be a table-top exercise. Other states, including Arizona and Hawaii, have guidelines but no mandated laws for drills. As a general rule, the best practice is to drill on all scenarios to improve the ability to respond.

OPTIONS-BASED APPROACHES FOR ACTIVE SHOOTER RESPONSE

In contrast to the common drills that teach and practice a specific response for preparing for and responding to multiple threats and hazards, such as lockdown, evacuation, or

shelter-in-place drills, options-based approacheslike Run Hide
Fight, Avoid Deny Defend, and A.L.I.C.E. provide multiple
response strategies to use in the event of a single threat, an
active shooter incident.[6] Active shooters are defined as "one
or more individuals actively engaged in killing or attempting
to kill people in a populated area."[7] Practices to prepare individuals for these events, also referred to as armed assailant or
active attacker/shooter drills, teach different tactics that can
be used as the situation requires.[8] The underlying rationale is
that active shooter events evolve quickly and unpredictably
and often end before law enforcement arrives, so more than
one response may be needed.[9]

There are many different variations of the options-based
approaches, although Run Hide Fight is the method that is
best known and has been used by the federal government
for responding to violence in the workplace and other settings.[10] "Run" refers to evacuating (or fleeing) the scene by
taking an accessible path to get out of harm's way, getting to
a safe location, and calling 911. Personal belongings such as
backpacks or purses should be left behind (though phones
and keys should be taken if quickly and easily accessible). If
possible, individuals may help others flee the scene safely.
Depending on the timing, individuals may need to run when
law enforcement already has arrived on the scene. In such
cases, they should keep their hands visible and follow the
directions being given by the officers, which may be issued
verbally or through physical cues such as hand signals. If
evacuation is not possible, the "hide" option involves finding a place out of the assailant's view that is protected, such
as behind a locked door in an area out of sight from the corridor, and remaining quiet. As a final option, if a person is in

imminent danger when the assailant has been able to gain access to that person's location, "fight" involves taking direct action to disrupt or stop the attacker through physical aggression, throwing items, or using makeshift weapons such as chairs, scissors, books, or fire extinguishers. It is important to note that the fight option is a last resort when no other alternatives exist to save lives.

The US Department of Education's *Guide for Developing High-Quality School Emergency Operations Plans* specifically includes the Run Hide Fight method, with information about training students and staff to flee the scene or to take cover in a safe location. It also discusses the last resort, if running and hiding are not options, of trying to disrupt or stop the shooter. The guide clarifies that this should never be required of a school employee, and that how each staff member chooses to respond if confronted by an active shooter is up to that person. Other options-based approaches, such as A.L.I.C.E. and Avoid Deny Defend, offer different variations.[11] Although various protocols exist, the steps are largely the same. For example, "avoid" is synonymous with "run," "deny" equates to "hide," and "defend" is similar to "fight."

Lockdown drills differ in a few ways from options-based approaches and more involved exercises. Lockdown drills entail practicing a specific procedure, such as securing quietly in a concealed area behind locked doors, whereas options-based approaches train people in multiple responses. Lockdown drills can be used to practice for *any* violent threat in the school building and are part of a broader all-hazards emergency response plan, whereas options-based approaches focus primarily on preparing specifically for an armed assailant in the immediate area. In addition, lockdown drills involve an announcement of the procedure to signal school staff and students to respond with previously learned procedures, whereas options-based approaches and functional and full-scale exercises may involve actors posing as assailants and the use of such props as airsoft guns, fake wounds, or stage blood to simulate a real event. Finally, lockdown drills include school staff and students, whereas some functional and full-scale exercises are geared more toward tactical preparedness, training, and collaboration for law enforcement, medical, and other first responders.[12]

HOW SHOULD DRILLS AND EXERCISES BE USED TO HELP SCHOOLS PREPARE FOR EMERGENCIES?

Engaging in exercises, including drills, to familiarize school staff, students, and community agencies with the emergency operations plan is an important part of preparing for crises before they happen. Decisions about drills and exercises should be made by multidisciplinary school safety and crisis teams comprising a mixture of administrators, school resource officers, facilities and planning personnel, communications specialists, school mental health professionals, nurses, and, if feasible and appropriate, teachers, students, and parents, in collaboration with community agencies such as law enforcement and other emergency response organizations. Such collaboration helps address the multiple issues, including preparation and training essentials, logistics, notification, and mental health needs, that should be considered when schools implement exercises and drills. These teams should follow state and local requirements in decision-making, and data on the threat and hazard vulnerabilities for the school and area should also guide decisions. For example, schools on the West Coast need to be prepared to respond in the event of an earthquake or a tsunami, whereas schools in the Northeast may need more practice in ice and snowstorm response. For all drills, planning must take into account students, staff, and visitors with disabilities or other accessibility or functional needs, including but not limited to different language comprehension skills, medication needs, or transportation needs.[13]

Exercises and drills should follow a progressive approach, starting with basic discussion-based exercises and only then advancing to more complex and involved operations. For example, a school might start with an orientation at the beginning of the school year to ensure that all school staff and students are taught the steps of the various emergency procedures. The school and district crisis teams then may engage in tabletop exercises to test the plan under different hypothetical scenarios. Emergency preparedness drills could be conducted monthly at different times of the day. The exercises then may introduce more functional components, such as blocking certain exit routes or scheduling at arrival time, to test preparedness in different situations. After each drill or exercise, the team should debrief and prepare an after-action report that reviews objectives and identifies any weaknesses to be addressed in a revised plan.[14] Full-scale exercises may take place after the proper planning with community agencies. The objectives of these exercises should be clear; for example, some may be conducted to train law enforcement officers or other first responders, while others may be undertaken to be sure school staff and students can perform the emergency preparedness procedures.[15] If the school decides to hold a full-scale exercise with actors pretending to be in a crisis situation, this intention should be fully disclosed in advance, and students and staff should be appropriately screened and their consent obtained for voluntary participation, particularly if the exercise involves exposure to highly sensorial experiences.[16]

Decision-makers must consider the costs and benefits of each proposed exercise in terms of financial resources, loss of instructional time, and human resources. The significant cost and planning involved in a full-scale exercise for an active shooter scenario may not be justified if a school has not first done the necessary tabletop exercises and lockdown drills to prepare. Alternatively, a school may have conducted multiple fire drills at the same time of day so that the procedure does not allow accurate testing of the plan in different situations. It is important that drills be conducted at different times of day—during lunch, after school arrival, during dismissal, and even during bell changes—which may require different procedures, such as evacuating offsite and reunifying with families. Feasibility, time, and resources all must be carefully considered when developing the exercise schedule. Finally, once decisions are made about the drills and exercises, there should be advance communication with school faculty and staff, as well as with parents, students, and community agencies, as to the purpose of the practices and the time frame and other specifics, such as location, so that all vested parties can be fully informed and notified that the exercise is not an actual emergency situation.[17]

Despite these recommendations, schools vary drastically in the practice of implementing drills. Many conduct lockdown drills first with orientation and then practice using a standard response, while others utilize approaches that prepare students and staff to engage by any means necessary, including active attack responses using books, cans, chairs, or other readily available items, to stop an armed assailant. These drills have become a commonplace yet highly controversial and polarized topic within the public discourse on school safety. The next chapter explores the arguments for and against conducting such drills in schools commonly raised in relation to these practices.

4

SHOULD WE OR SHOULDN'T WE?
ARGUMENTS FOR AND AGAINST LOCKDOWN DRILLS

Key Takeaways

- There are many arguments for and against conducting lockdown drills with students.
- Proponents argue that lockdown drills increase self-protection skills and perceptions of emergency preparedness without increasing anxiety, are effective in saving lives, and are consistent with federal guidance and best practices for emergency operations plans to be effective.
- Critics argue that lockdown drills teach people to be helpless behind locked doors, spend resources on statistically rare events, divulge school protocols to potential perpetrators, and have wide variations in practice without adequate research support.
- It is important for schools to use practices to increase preparedness while not causing harm.

Leading school safety authorities, including the US Department of Education,[1] Safe Havens International,[2] the "I Love U Guys" Foundation,[3] the National Association of School Psychologists,[4] and the National School Safety and Security Services,[5] assert that emergency operations plans must be practiced with drills and exercises. Practicing allows school staff, students, and emergency responders to familiarize themselves with the procedures outlined in the plan so that they know what to do in the event of a threat or hazard, and to improve muscle memory. In fact, one of the major responsibilities of school and district safety teams is to engage in the planning and practice of drills.

Despite these recommendations, lockdown drills (which are often erroneously equated with active shooter drills, options-based approaches, and full-scale exercises) have been at the center of attention and controversy in recent years. As with many contentious topics, people have assumed the role of either advocate or abolitionist when it comes to lockdown drills. In this chapter, we explore the commonly offered talking points as to why these practices should or should not take place. We also discuss the confusion between lockdown drills, options-based approaches, and highly sensorial exercises. Table 4.1 outlines the major arguments for and against conducting lockdown drills. Throughout the chapter, we provide evidence-based support and counterarguments to each point listed in the table in an effort to better understand the conversation around these practices.

ARGUMENTS FOR CONDUCTING LOCKDOWN DRILLS

Related to the point made earlier that emergency operations plans must be rehearsed and applied, best practice guidance on emergency preparedness from the federal government specifies conducting lockdown (and other) drills. The US Department of Homeland Security (DHS), for example, published an extensive document on preparedness practices and

Table 4.1   Arguments for and against lockdown drills

Support for/Rationale	Criticisms of and Arguments Against
• Emergency operations plans must be exercised (through drills) to be effective. • Lockdown drills are consistent with federal best practice guidelines (e.g., those issued by the US Department of Education or FEMA). • Drills increase student and staff self-protection skills and muscle memory. • Participating in lockdown drills enhances perceptions of emergency preparedness. • Properly conducted lockdown drills can enhance preparedness without increasing anxiety. • Properly conducted lockdown procedures (securing behind locked door) are effective in saving lives.	• Teaching people to hide behind a locked door may lead to feelings of helplessness (they may be "sitting ducks" if confronted by an armed assailant). • Focusing time and resources on statistically rare events such as school shootings may take away from preparedness for other. more likely threats and hazards. • Having students participate in these drills could divulge school preparedness protocols to potential perpetrators. • Lack of federal guidance and vague state guidance lead to wide variation in how drills are conducted (e.g., unannounced or with a highly sensorial component). • Drills may lead to physical or psychological harm to participants. • There is a lack of research supporting the effectiveness of drills.

evaluation in 2020, emphasizing how vital drills and exercises are in strengthening communities to engage in all aspects of emergency preparedness.[6] Specific to schools, the US Department of Education offers a pair of guides that include lockdowns as a specific, critical operational function (the relevant sections of the guides are referred to as functional annexes) for schools to include in their emergency operations plans.[7] Both documents emphasize the importance of drills and exercises to ensure that school faculty and staff, students, parents, and community representatives understand their respective roles.

The Readiness and Emergency Management for Schools (REMS) Technical Assistance Center similarly includes drills and exercises as part of schools' mitigation strategies.[8] *Mitigation* is an aspect of preparedness that focuses on actions schools can take to reduce or eliminate death, injury, and property damage resulting from a crisis event; training and conducting drills can help keep the community safe and minimize these consequences. The *Final Report of the U.S. Federal Commission on School Safety* also indicates that each school's plan should include multiple functions (with lockdowns included in the list) and hazards, and that the plan must be practiced so that students, teachers, and administrators know their roles and responsibilities.[9] Therefore, conducting lockdown drills as part of comprehensive planning and preparedness efforts for multiple threats and hazards is a widely agreed-upon best practice.

Another argument for conducting lockdown drills is to teach students and staff necessary self-protection skills and increase perceptions of preparedness. Drawing from the larger field, one review indicated that 66 percent of studies of disaster education preparedness programs in which a variety of discussion-based and drill components were used with children showed positive outcomes, including increased knowledge and awareness of disaster response and improved attitudes toward preparedness.[10] As applied to earthquake preparedness, the combination of lectures—providing information about this natural disaster and how to respond—and drills—offering a brief overview of behavioral steps and then practicing them—resulted in the highest knowledge scores among a sample of upper elementary school students in Israel.[11] Several studies focusing on lockdown drills specifically have demonstrated that children's participation in lockdown drills can increase their skill in implementing the lockdown procedures.[12] Collectively, the findings indicate that children improve their knowledge and skill mastery after participating in training and lockdown drills.

It is important that people not only know what to do but also perceive themselves to be prepared. According to protection motivation theory, people are motivated to take action to safeguard themselves against harm based on the weighing of vulnerability, risk (e.g., the likelihood of a threat's occurrence), and potential consequences (e.g., severity) against the perceived benefits of engaging in protective behavior, their self-efficacy (the belief that one has the ability to take the actions needed to protect oneself), and response efficacy (whether the actions will be effective in reducing or eliminating the threat).[13] Therefore, a goal of teaching and practicing emergency preparedness procedures such as lockdowns is to increase beliefs or perceptions about being prepared to engage in protective actions. In our large-scale study of lockdown drills in an urban school district, we found that participation in training and drills led to increased perceptions of preparedness on the part of both students and educators.[14]

In teaching and practicing these skills and increasing preparedness, it is important not to create undue anxiety or arouse fears on the part of participants for their own safety. Although protection motivation theory suggests that experiencing a sense of vulnerability and risk actually motivates people to engage in protective behavior, it is undesirable to create situations that cause students or staff to experience undue anxiety and stress or to feel unsafe in schools. Highly sensorial simulations and full-scale exercises are much more likely to elicit these responses. In contrast, research has found that when drills are conducted in accordance with best practices, anxiety typically remains unchanged or is even lowered, suggesting that the lockdown drills are not contributing to consistent, problematic anxiety and fears for student participants.

Beyond skill mastery and their contribution to perceptions of preparedness, perhaps the most compelling argument for conducting lockdown drills is to save lives. Similar to evacuating to escape from a fire or wearing a seat belt to protect from injury or death in a car accident, securing behind a locked door has been identified as the most effective way to prevent injury or death during an active shooter situation.[15] According to testimony provided to the Sandy Hook Advisory Commission, no one has been injured or killed behind a locked door because the lock failed.[16] If people have participated in lockdown drills and practiced locking the door and getting out of sight, their improved muscle memory can make this a more automated response, which may be vital in taking the steps necessary to prevent injury or death.

ARGUMENTS AGAINST CONDUCTING LOCKDOWN DRILLS

One of the criticisms of lockdown drills is that teaching students and staff to hide behind locked doors may make them "sitting ducks," a term often used in news reports that discuss bringing options-based training to schools.[17] The concern is that hiding will make people vulnerable and more at risk of being killed or injured if faced with an armed assailant such as an active shooter.[18] Therefore, options-based or multi-option approaches such as A.L.I.C.E., Run Hide Fight, or Avoid Deny Defend are being used increasingly to empower people with a survival mindset and to train individuals to use a variety of options, including running or fleeing the scene and barricading doors, actively resisting or fighting an armed assailant resorted to only when no other good options exist. A further argument for options-based approaches is that law enforcement personnel have used distraction techniques successfully to stop an incident and save lives. Indeed, the actions of evacuation, hiding, or acting against the assailant are part of the prevailing response to an active shooter designed by DHS for use in workplace settings.[19] Since the Sandy Hook shooting, it also has been applied to K–12 schools.[20]

Only a few studies have been conducted on options-based approaches. In an experimental study of a simulated shooting with adult participants in an A.L.I.C.E training session, the options-based approach simulation was completed in a shorter period of time and fewer people were "shot" with airsoft guns, which the authors suggested indicated greater survivability.[21] A separate study of video and audio simulations with school staff members, however, found that those who had completed options-based training performed worse than those who had not been trained.[22] Specifically, they misjudged almost twice as many critical action steps, such as attacking anyone depicted as having a gun, regardless of the scenario, or choosing to evacuate even if doing so would increase danger. The scant research available therefore is inconclusive and does not address the involvement of children in these approaches. One exception is a study of fourth through twelfth graders who participated in discussion-based lessons on the A.L.I.C.E. protocol. The researchers found that most students, over 85 percent, felt more prepared and less scared or expressed no changes in such perceptions after learning the options. The students who felt more scared also were likely to be fearful of other prepared-ness procedures, such as tornado drills and stranger danger drills.[23] More research is needed to examine the effectiveness and impact of multi-option approaches, particularly when students are participating and a drill component is involved.

Although the previous criticisms, such as not teaching people in the options-based approaches, are specific to lock-down drills, most of the other arguments are about active shooter or armed assailant drills, which often encompass lock-downs. Lockdowns differ from simulations and options-based approaches, and the National Association of School Psychologists, National Association of Resource Officers, and Safe and Sound Schools have called for accuracy in differentiating between these drills and exercises.[24] Since lockdowns often are incorrectly lumped together with active shooter drills, it is important to address these criticisms.

Another related concern raised about lockdown drills when the focus is on armed assailants is that allocating time and resources to statistically rare events such as school shootings may divert resources from other, more compre-hensive school safety planning and preparedness efforts for multiple hazards. The joint statement from Everytown for Gun Safety, the American Federation of Teachers, and the National Education Association, for example, raises the issue that for-profit companies charge tens of thousands of dollars to provide active shooter training when the funds could be spent on preventive approaches such as threat assessment, employing more school-based mental health professionals, upgrading security, and improving the school climate.[25] One report indicated that a school district in California paid more than $32,000 over three years for A.L.I.C.E. training. Another indicated that the training cost a school district $56,000 in one year, plus $25,000 in each of the next two years.[26] In contrast, some programs, such as the Standard Response Protocol, provide online training resources for lockdowns and other response protocols to K–12 schools at no cost.[27]

Critics of lockdown drills also suggest that involving students may be problematic because it may divulge school preparedness protocols to potential perpetrators of school shootings. This argument does not take into account that locking a door creates a time barrier, which will be an obstacle whether or not a perpetrator knows that this is part of the protocol. In addition, the reality is that only a miniscule percentage of students might go on to engage in an act of massive violence against the school; the far greater likelihood is that teaching thousands of students to protect themselves outweighs the chance that training in these emergency protocols would give potential perpetrators information they otherwise would not know.

A criticism with clear policy implications is the very wide variability in the ways in which schools practice drills. There is no federal standard relevant to these practices, and statutes concerning drills often are vague; thus practices vary dramatically from school to school.[28] Multiple media reports exist of drills that included gunshots to make the experience more real or of schools telling teachers there was an active shooter when it only was a drill.[29] There also are reports on the use of stage blood and fake guns as police pose as active shooters (with student volunteers playing the role of victims).[30]

Conducting drills that simulate the actual experience of being threatened by a shooter (e.g., with actors, gunshots, and stage blood) has raised concern about the potential psychological and physical harm that may ensue. Empirical research on this topic is very limited, and although the evidence on lockdown drills to date does not support the contention that carefully conducted drills elicit stress and fear, studies have not been conducted on the more sensorial approaches that are more likely to be traumatizing. In options-based approaches that teach students and staff to directly confront an assailant, there is added concern about increased harm and more deaths.[31] These fears about the possible effects of these practices have led to calls to end active shooter drills (and, by extension, lockdown drills).[32] Professional organizations, however, including the National Association of School Psychologists, the National Association of School Resource Officers, and the American Academy of Pediatrics, rather than opposing all drills, have provided best practice guidance on conducting drills and have advocated for including this guidance in legislation.[33]

Finally, critics point to an alarming lack of research on the practice of drills, even though they are conducted routinely in schools every day across the country. The American Academy of Pediatrics has advocated for funding to research the effectiveness, goals, and potential unintended consequences of drills.[34] Although several recent studies have begun to examine these practices, because of the great variability in implementation across schools, several specific components have not been carefully evaluated. When it comes to the safety of children at school, it is clear that schools, families, and the general public do not want to wait for tragedy to strike and instead demand action. At the same time, there is understandable concern that the rush to do something already has done, and could potentially do more, harm than good if drills are not implemented carefully and according to best practices.

FINDING COMMON GROUND

Implementing practices that increase preparedness while not causing harm is critical to reach the ultimate and common goal of saving lives. There are impassioned arguments on both sides of the issue as to whether or not lockdown drills should be conducted with students. The arguments against lockdown drills listed in table 4.1 and discussed in this chapter include the suggestion that such practices teach people to be helpless behind locked doors, misallocate resources toward statistically rare events, divulge school protocols to potential perpetrators, lack clear-cut federal and state guidance, increase the potential for physical or psychological harm, and lack research support. Arguments in favor of conducting lockdown drills with students include increasing self-protection skills and perceptions of emergency preparedness without increasing anxiety, improving effectiveness in saving lives, and following federal guidance and best practices regarding the need to practice emergency operations plans for them to be effective. The tremendous variability in the implementation of drills and confusion over the terminology, resulting in the conflation of different practices—active shooter drills might consist of a lockdown, at one end of the spectrum, or, at the other end, a highly sensorial simulation during which people are empowered to flee the area, take cover and hide, or throw objects and use physical force in an attempt to stop the perpetrator—add fuel to the controversy. One thing that most agree on is that schools are using variations of drills routinely—often, but not always, by state mandate—and that research has lagged behind. Part II of this book explores evidence on lockdown drills with regard to their effects on students (chapter 5) and preparation for faculty and staff (chapter 6). Chapter 7 addresses the issue of whether lockdowns meet the ultimate goal of keeping people safe.

II

WHAT DOES THE RESEARCH SAY?

5

FOR STUDENTS
ARE WE TRAINING OR TRAUMATIZING?

Key Takeaways

- There are different ways to assess the impacts of lockdown drills on students, including evaluating changes in their anxiety levels, fear, and perceptions of risk, safety, and preparedness before and after the practice.
- Self-reported anxiety levels have been found to be the same or lower after students participate in a drill compared to before it.
- Results are mixed as to whether participating in lockdown or active shooter drills makes students feel more fearful or less safe.
- Students overwhelmingly report feeling more prepared to respond to emergencies as a result of participating in drills.
- School administrators and policymakers must carefully balance the potential risks of students participating in these practices with the benefits that can be gained from doing so.

Students attending primary and secondary schools in the United States after April 20, 1999, have become known as "Generation Columbine"—youth who do not know a world without lockdown drills, bulletproof backpacks, and other strategies designed to keep them safe in the event the very

worst day ever happens on their campus.[1] Including the now
infamous attack at the Jefferson County, Colorado, high
school, there were fifty-one school-based mass shootings
between 1999 and 2019.[2] These tragedies claimed the lives of
185 students and educators and left 246 others with physical injuries. Not included in these statistics, however, are the
countless others who were present on school grounds during
the attack and who, while not bearing physical reminders of
that day, suffered psychological and emotional trauma as a
result of their experiences.

An issue of concern is the potential impact of the practices designed to prepare students to respond to these types
of emergencies, such as drills, on the well-being of those who
participate in them. Drills that are especially realistic have
raised concerns that these practices go too far and are traumatizing students.[3] The potential harms mentioned include
anxiety, depression, posttraumatic stress disorder (PTSD), and
declines in academic performance.[4] Others have argued that
even the mildest drills can make children feel unsafe.[5] As a
result, there have been repeated calls to end these practices,
despite the reality that mass shootings in schools continue to
occur, highlighting the need to be prepared to respond.

Much of the discourse about emergency preparedness drills
from vested stakeholders, including parents, school administrators and staff, researchers, and the media, has focused on
the negative impacts of these practices.[6] Unless the positive
impacts of drills also are considered, however, a significant
piece of the conversation is missing, which yields an incom-
plete picture of the overall effectiveness of the practices. In
this chapter, we consider the relationship between potential
impacts, including increased (or decreased) anxiety or fear
and perceptions of safety and preparedness, and participation

in drills and training as it pertains to students. We also explore some broader considerations about the potential impacts and benefits of involving students in emergency preparedness efforts.

ANXIETY

Among children and adolescents, anxiety disorders are the most common mental health concern,[7] with over 7 percent of US youth between the ages of three and seventeen having a formal diagnosis.[8] Youth who are exposed to school- and community-based violence in particular have been found to be three times more likely to develop anxiety disorders than those who have lower exposure.[9] It has been suggested that even the very threat of an emergency can have a negative impact on anxiety levels among children,[10] and, by extension, so too could associated preparedness efforts. High-intensity drills, for example, may increase anxiety among students because they can evoke perceptions that the world is not safe.[11] For students with anxiety, stress-related disorders, or other psychological or behavioral health problems, these reactions may be exacerbated when practices are not conducted in a trauma-informed manner.[12] As a result, administrators and school safety teams are challenged to best to prepare students for a crisis without eliciting, provoking, or exacerbating anxiety or other reactions.[13]

Just two studies to date, however, have specifically assessed potential changes to anxiety levels relative to active participation in a lockdown drill. In one study of seventy-four students in the fourth, fifth, and sixth grades, researchers found that students who participated in preparedness training and a subsequent intruder drill did not differ in their state anxiety from those who practiced origami.[14] State anxiety refers to temporary or short-lived emotions of worry, tension, or nervousness, whereas trait anxiety is the prolonged and stable presence of such feelings.[15] As the researchers observed, none of the students during the drill expressed, either verbally or through their body language or behavior, being distressed or negatively affected by participating.

In a separate study, measurements of anxiety were collected from more than six hundred students in a rural high school in New York state approximately one week before and immediately after (during the debriefing period) a lockdown drill.[16] Although the students reported low anxiety prior to taking part in the drill, their reported levels were even lower after the drill. Their reported well-being, which represents feelings free of anxiety (e.g., calm, content, relaxed), was found to be higher after the drill than before it. In other words, students did not exhibit greater anxiety after participating in the drill; rather, they actually reported feeling better overall, which may be a result of feeling more prepared. A key takeaway of both studies is that lockdown drills conducted in accordance with best practices were found not to increase anxiety levels among student participants and may even have had positive effects by empowering them with the skills necessary to respond in an emergency.

FEAR AND PERCEIVED RISK

Researchers also have considered how participation in active shooter or lockdown drills can influence perceptions beyond anxiety, including fear and perceived risk. Although there is considerable debate within the academic literature about *how* anxiety and fear differ, there is agreement that they are distinct from one another.[17] Researchers also have contended that fear and perceived risk, while related, are conceptually different.[18] To have a complete picture of the impact of drills on participants, all must be considered.

In the broader school safety literature, fear among students has been found to increase with the occurrence of school shootings[19] and with the presence of security guards and metal detectors.[20] Some researchers have suggested that participating in drills designed to prepare students for active shooter events can lead to the same outcome. One retrospective study of college students that asked them about their experiences with active shooter drills in high school suggested that both fear and perceived risk were higher among those who had participated in such a practice than among those who had not.[21] This study did not account for the type of practice that was conducted (e.g., tabletop, drill, functional exercise), and therefore the findings cannot necessarily be used to understand the effects of lockdown drills more specifically owing to the variability in these approaches. In a separate study assessing the effects of training that used a video about school shootings, researchers found that self-reported fear among college students increased after they watched the recording. The average level of fear, however, was low at both measurement points (before and after viewing) among all participants, regardless of whether they watched the training video or the documentary on the Sandy Hook Elementary School shooting perpetrator (control group).[22] In other words, these groups did not vary significantly in their levels of fear, suggesting that the specific impact of viewing the training video may have been overstated.

Fear related to drills and training may be susceptible to multiple factors beyond just the practices themselves. One study considering emergency preparedness efforts found that students who were scared of other response strategies (fire and tornado drills, stranger danger) also were more likely to express being scared and worried after participating in training in the A.L.I.C.E. protocol, but that they generally were no more fearful of active shooter drills than they were of other practices.[23] This finding was consistent among all participants who completed the training, with a vast majority of students—89 percent of elementary school respondents and 94 percent of those in junior high and high school—not reporting increased fear after participating in the training. Students at the junior high and high school levels were, however, more likely to express feeling worried if they also believed there was an increased likelihood they would have to use what they learned in the training in a real event, a finding that highlights the important relationship between fear and perceived risk of victimization. Although this study did not assess such perceptions in connection with an actual drill, its findings highlight important considerations related to students' fears regarding emergency response practices and the need to conduct such practices in a trauma-informed manner to offset any potential adverse reactions.

PERCEPTIONS OF SAFETY

How safe students view themselves and their school environment is another way in which the potential impacts of lockdowns drills can be assessed. Previous research has suggested that, similar to student fear, physical measures such as the presence of security officers or metal detectors also negatively affect their perceptions of safety at school.[24] The literature on the relationship between perceived safety and lockdown or active shooter drills shows mixed results. In one text poll conducted with a national sample of youth (defined in the study as individuals aged fourteen to twenty-four), approximately 53 percent of participants indicated that active shooter drills specifically made them feel safer as a result of making them more prepared to respond (discussed further in the next section).[25] Nearly one out of every four students, however, expressed that the practices did not make them feel safer. Instead, they reported that the drills made them targets, that the protocols practiced would not actually stop the shooter, or that they did not provide sufficient comparisons to prepare for a real-world situation since, for example, people would not be as calm in an actual emergency as they were during the drill. As with other studies, these findings are considered broadly in the context of active shooter drills and do not account for differences in protocols or training that the respondents may have encountered.

Other studies have accounted for such disparities in experience by examining perceptions of safety in the context of specific protocols or trainings. In the A.L.I.C.E. study mentioned earlier, the researchers found that between 89 percent and 95 percent of the students who participated in the training reported either feeling safer or experiencing no changes in perceived safety after learning about the protocol.[26] Those who felt less safe also reported feeling more scared of other types of emergency preparedness practices. In a separate study assessing the effects of an intruder drill, students who participated in training and in the practice did not differ significantly in terms of their perceptions of school safety from those who did not.[27]

In a larger study conducted in the course of implementing a standardized, all hazards emergency response protocol in a large urban school district in upstate New York, researchers considered whether participating in multiple lockdown drills and preparedness training had an impact on perceptions of school safety.[28] Data were collected at three time points—at baseline (the start of the project), after an initial lockdown drill, and after training and a second lockdown drill—from more than 10,000 students. The findings indicated that perceived safety at the school and in various areas within it (classrooms, cafeteria, hallways) decreased over the course of the project. While this drop in perceived safety may have resulted from participation in the training and drills, the authors could not conclude that it could be solely attributable to these practices because during the course of the project, several students were killed in community violence–related incidents, which may have affected perceptions of how safe the schools were. Previous research similarly has found that the location of schools in high-crime and poverty areas, such as those in the upstate New York study, has a negative impact on students' perceptions of school safety.[29] This finding highlights the need to consider not only the correlation between lockdown drills and perceived school safety but also the interplay with other factors that may be affecting perceptions of school safety. Although participating in lockdown drills may not always produce positive outcomes related to perceptions of school safety among students, the potential trade-offs, such as skill acquisition, must be considered in deciding not only whether to conduct these practices but also how to do so. The adoption of trauma-informed approaches and best practices may help mitigate subsequent anxieties about school safety, though more research is needed to fully understand the potential effects of these approaches.

PERCEIVED PREPAREDNESS

Though studies have found disparate findings related to anxiety, fear and risk, and perceptions of safety in relation to active shooter drills, the available research does agree on one significant conclusion: participating in training and drills makes students feel more prepared to respond in emergencies.[30] This finding holds across different study designs and different protocols. For instance, more than half the students in the text poll survey referenced earlier who actually participated in an active shooter drill reported that the practice made them feel more prepared to respond in a real situation.[31] This was a separate observation from how safe they felt: though they believed themselves to be more prepared, they did not believe drills served to prevent shootings from occurring in the first place.

The importance of the preparedness aspect emerges even when specific types or modes of training are examined. For instance, students have reported feeling more prepared to respond to a shooting on their campus after viewing a training video than before viewing the film.[32] In another study, nearly 87 percent of junior high and high school students reported feeling more prepared to respond to a violent incident after completing discussion-based training with their teachers.[33] How often students are trained also can affect such perceptions, with more frequent participation in training sessions leading to greater feelings of preparedness.

Only two studies published to date have considered how participation in actual lockdown drills affects students' perception of preparedness.[34] In addition to collecting data on perceived school safety during the standardization of a large district's response plan, the researchers also asked students how prepared they felt to respond to the five different scenarios— lockdown, lockout, evacuate, hold, and shelter—that made up the new protocol. For all five emergency situations, students expressed feeling more prepared to respond after participating in the training and both lockdown drills. When responses to each emergency were examined separately, students expressed feeling most ready to respond in a lockdown compared to the other four scenarios, a finding that further highlights the importance of preparing for a specific threat and assessing both perceptions of the practice and the effectiveness of the drill itself. It also is possible that feelings of preparedness may help mitigate, at least in part, some of the adverse reactions students have to these drills, including increases in fear levels and perceived risk or decreases in perceived safety.

SOME BROADER CONSIDERATIONS

The findings of the studies discussed in this chapter highlight some important considerations with regard to the effects of drills and training on students. First, students experience a host of emotions or perceptual changes related to these practices, from anxiety and fear to perceived safety and preparedness. Conducting both drills and training in a developmentally and age-appropriate manner and following guidance in best practices can help ensure that students are able to prepare for emergencies and gain the knowledge and skills for a crisis response without experiencing any major negative psychological impacts. Similarly, combining training with drills can help reduce fears and anxiety over potential threats while increasing skill acquisition as students learn the reasons behind the steps they are asked to complete, which may increase their confidence in the practice and in their abilities to respond if needed.[35]

Second, how the drills are conducted also may affect how students feel about them. Many of the research studies discussed in this chapter did not take into account the specific protocol used or how the practice was conducted when they assessed potential psychological impacts. Highly sensorial drills that include traumatic stimuli such as stage blood or sounds of simulated gunfire can potentially increase anxiety and lead to heightened perceptions that schools are unsafe. They also may inflate students' perceived risk of a shooting happening at their school, which can increase feelings of stress or anxiety. As well, practices or protocols that are not fully grounded in evidence-based recommendations may contribute to adverse reactions and emotional distress resulting from the drills.[36]

Finally, although some studies discussed here suggested the presence of negative psychological impacts, including increased fear and reduced perceived safety, it is possible that these effects are immediate rather than prolonged reactions to the practices and will fade with repeated practice. It also begs the question of whether these negative impacts, which typically are concentrated among a small number of students rather than being commonly experienced by the majority, are counterbalanced by the benefits to be gained with respect to increased emergency preparedness and confidence in responding. As illustrated in figure 5.1, students in one study described here reported perceiving their schools to be less safe as the academic year and the preparedness project progressed, but reported increases in feeling prepared to respond to emergencies as reflected in increased confidence

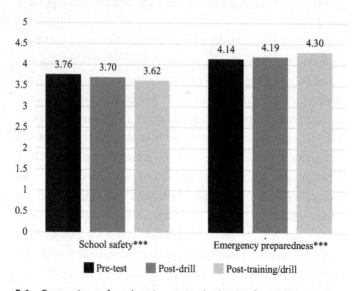

5.1 Comparison of students' perceived school safety and emergency preparedness prior to and after participating in lockdown drills and training. *Note.* Three asterisks (***) represent a statistically significant difference between the different time intervals. Students were asked to rate their agreement on a five-point Likert scale (1 = Strongly Disagree to 5 = Strongly Agree). For school safety, students were asked to rate their agreement with the statement "I feel safe" at school, in the classroom, in the cafeteria, and in the hallway; these responses were summed, then collapsed into an aggregate measure. Similarly, for emergency preparedness, students were asked to assess "I know what to do during a" lockout, lockdown, evacuation, and shelter-in-place and hold-in-place. A composite measure for emergency preparedness was subsequently created from these responses.

in their abilities, which potentially mitigates such losses. Protection motivation theory may help explain this dynamic. According to the theory, people need to feel some level of threat, risk, or vulnerability to engage in protective behavior.[37] When a threat is present, an individual will evaluate it ("Is this likely to happen? How bad will it be?") relative to the potential benefits of engaging in the protective behavior ("Will this behavior be an effective response to the threat? Can I take the necessary action to protect myself and others?"). As long as it is accompanied by increased preparedness, in terms of both perceptions of behavior and perceptions of learned skills, some degree of fear or worry about violence or threats may be expected and actually helpful in motivating people to protect themselves and others, as might learning (by way of training and drills) how to do so. Therefore, the increases in perceived preparedness exhibited in figure 5.1 may reflect students believing they are less safe at school and taking action through participating in drills and training to mitigate such feelings. These considerations should be discussed not only within the research community but also among vested stakeholders charged with keeping students safe and protecting their well-being. More research evaluating the effects of these practices is needed, both short-term effects, such as psychological reactions, and long-term effects, such as the impact of these practices on school performance and school avoidance, and the positive and negative effects must be introduced into the conversation to have a complete and well-rounded discussion about how best to prepare students for emergencies that may occur in their schools.

Organizations such as the American Academy of Pediatrics stress the importance of including children and adolescents in preparedness efforts, including lockdown drills.[38] This is important not only to ensure that the students understand how to respond and are prepared to respond in an emergency but also to help them build a sense of resiliency. Understanding how to respond can help protect students' well-being and minimize both physical and psychological harms. All who are responsible for students' well-being, however, including school administrators and safety teams, must be mindful of the potential psychological risks and unintended consequences of involving students in the practices. Additionally, it is important to consider how the practices affect the educators—not just faculty but also school staff and administrators—charged with keeping students safe, as this too may affect how students process and understand emergency preparedness efforts. We explore this topic further in the next chapter.

6

FOR FACULTY AND STAFF
BUILDING COOPERATION
AND COLLABORATION

Key Takeaways

- Research examining educators' perceived safety at school has found it to be high and unaffected by participating in lockdown drills.
- Perceived emergency preparedness, on the other hand, is improved after educators take part in training and drills.
- Educators differ in both perceived safety and perceived preparedness based on their roles, so training plans should account for these group differences.
- Emergency preparedness efforts should be supplemented with other learning opportunities, including training with first responders and instruction in emergency first aid.
- Efforts to provide guidance on emergency response plans should be ongoing rather than conducted only at the start of the school year.

Although the focus of schools is largely on the students they serve, students are not the only individuals who must be prepared for emergencies. Faculty and staff take on an even more important role because they are charged with not only educating and caring for students but also with preparing them for crisis events and protecting them should such events occur. Understanding educators' perceptions of emergency response protocols, including lockdown drills, is vital to assessing a school's overall preparedness efforts. If school personnel do not feel ready to respond, it is unlikely they will be able to help themselves or the students. Just as they must have certain supplies, such as chalk, paper, and pencils, to do their jobs effectively, they must have the skills necessary to act in an emergency situation.

In this chapter, we examine faculty, staff, and administrator perceptions of lockdown drills as assessed in the scholarly research. Although this body of literature, like the literature on students' perceptions, is quite limited, the available studies provide important insight into how educators perceive these practices in the context of safety and emergency preparedness efforts. We explore how such perceptions may vary based on the role of the individual, as differences have been found between faculty, who work directly with students, and staff and administrators, who serve the school in a broader capacity. We also consider what changes these groups feel should be made to enable them be as prepared as possible for school-based emergency situations, and how safety and response practices can instill confidence in educators that, individually and collectively, they are prepared to keep schools safe.

THE IMPACT OF DRILLS ON PERCEPTIONS OF SAFETY

Educators' perceptions of school safety can be affected by security-based policies and practices. Physical security measures, such as cameras, controlled building access, door locks, and visitor passes, have been found to correlate with greater feelings of perceived safety,[1] as has the presence of school resources officers.[2] Less is known about how safety perceptions are affected by nonphysical security measures such as lockdown drills. Understanding such perceptions is important because, in the words of one researcher, "safety is the pivotal component of crisis management."[3]

Just one study to date has assessed teacher perceptions relative to actual participation in lockdown drills.[4] Using survey data collected at three time points—at baseline (the start of the project), after a first lockdown drill, and after training and a second lockdown drill—in a large urban school district in New York, researchers considered whether participating in such practices had any influence on how faculty, staff, and administrators perceived safety at their school. The findings revealed that perceived safety in this particular sample, which included approximately one thousand respondents at each of the three time points, did not differ across time points. In other words, perceived school safety, which was particularly high within the sample to begin with, was not significantly affected, either positively or negatively, by participating in the training or lockdown drills.

Administrators were more likely than faculty members to report feeling safe at school, while staff were less likely to do so. School safety is considered a leadership issue, with those at the top responsible for making decisions about how best to plan and practice for possible emergencies.[5] Teachers have the most direct contact with students and often are considered to be the "first line of school safety," meaning they may have earlier awareness of potential problems and greater insight into who might be involved or affected, knowledge that can be used to formulate possible solutions.[6] If schools and their leadership are viewed as prepared, educators' perceived safety also may increase, and this increased confidence may be passed on to the students. Similarly, providing training has been found to increase comfort levels among teachers while helping to decrease their anxiety,[7] all of which may have an impact on perceptions of school safety.

THE IMPACT OF DRILLS ON PERCEIVED PREPAREDNESS

One area of focus in the research on educators and lockdown drills has been emergency preparedness, a necessary ingredient for response plans to be as effective as possible.[8] Preparedness levels also may correlate with perceived safety, but it is important to note that these are different concepts. *Safety* can be thought of as an individual's assessment of personal risk of danger, injury, or loss. Conversely, *preparedness* refers to how confident an individual feels about his or her ability to respond to said danger or how knowledgeable that person is about the appropriate procedures.

In the context of emergency response practices, individuals' perceived level of preparedness is contingent on several factors. First, the presence of an active shooter protocol or lockdown policy has been found to correspond to increased levels of perceived preparedness.[9] The more confidence individuals have in their school's emergency plans, the more prepared they perceive themselves to be because the necessary protocols are in place.[10] Second, participating in training in the emergency response plan improves feelings of preparedness. The more individuals practice the plan, the more confident they feel about being able to respond in a crisis as needed.[11] Moreover, practicing the procedure can help improve their recollection about how to respond and the specific steps of the protocol.[12] Finally, conducting drills has been found to correlate positively with increased perceptions of emergency preparedness. Creating the opportunity to practice the skills taught in training can improve a person's perceived likelihood of being able to execute them accurately during an actual emergency. Collectively, the more knowledgeable educators are about how to respond, the more confident they will feel about being able to do so in an actual crisis.

As with school safety, just one study—the assessment of the impact of lockdown drills among educators in one New York school district, mentioned earlier—examined perceived emergency preparedness in conjunction with these practices.[13] This study evaluated how prepared faculty, staff, and administrators in the thirty schools in the district felt relative to five different emergency scenarios—lockdown, lockout, evacuate, shelter in place, and hold in place. Schools were trained in these five scenarios, which are the emergency annexes of the Standard Response Protocol (SRP) from the "I Love U Guys" Foundation,[14] as part of a districtwide standardization of preparedness efforts. Preparedness was assessed at three time points—at the start of the project, after the first drill but before any training had taken place, and after training in the SRP and going through a second lockdown drill.

Collectively, the educators' perceived overall emergency preparedness (a combined measure of all five scenarios) was greater after they had completed training and participated in the second lockdown drill than at either of the other two survey time points. When the scenarios are examined separately, respondents collectively expressed feeling more knowledgeable about how to respond specifically to a lockdown, lockout, evacuation, shelter-in-place call, and hold-in-place call after the training and second drill than they did at the start of the project or after the first practice. Important differences were uncovered when the results were broken out according to the role—faculty, staff, or administrator—of the respondent. Administrators did not differ in their expressed familiarity with the procedures across time points, and their reported knowledge about how to respond to each scenario was higher than that of both faculty and staff at all three time intervals. (Notably, a separate study found that the more prepared teachers perceived their administration to be, the more likely to be able to respond in an active shooter situation the teachers perceived themselves to be,[15] further highlighting the importance of preparedness from the top down.) Faculty reported greater familiarity with how to respond to the lockout, shelter-in-place, and hold-in-place calls after training and the second drill compared to the other two time points; they did not, however, differ significantly in their familiarity with responding to lockdowns or evacuations. Staff, on the other hand, reported significantly greater knowledge about how to respond in each of the five scenarios after participating in the training and second lockdown drill compared to their responses at the other two survey points.

These findings highlight important considerations for school administrators and safety teams tasked with implementing and assessing emergency preparedness practices. In

New York, where the research study was conducted, schools are required to conduct four lockdown and eight evacuation (fire) drills annually.[16] It is therefore likely that faculty's familiarity with how to respond to these two scenarios did not significantly change because they already were accustomed to practicing them. Instead, familiarity increased for those scenarios—lockout, shelter in place, and hold in place—for which they did not regularly practice, highlighting the importance of schools conducting drills for all emergency scenarios they have plans for. Although staff work in the same building, they may not always participate in the drills alongside administrators, faculty, and students. Observations made by the researchers during the course of the drills highlighted that certain school employees, including cafeteria workers and custodial staff, continued their daily tasks during the drill rather than participating in the practice. As such, it is likely that their familiarity increased as a result of the training, which introduced them to the response protocols. This observation also highlights the importance of including all school-based personnel, not just those who work more directly with students, in the preparedness practices to continue fostering confidence in the response strategies. Since crises do not discriminate based on an individual's role, it is imperative that everyone in the building receive the proper training and practice.

IDENTIFYING OPPORTUNITIES FOR IMPROVEMENT

Regardless of how prepared individuals believed themselves to be or how confident they were in their ability to respond in a lockdown situation, a number of opportunities for improvement were highlighted by educators across different studies (see table 6.1 for a summary of these recommendations). One of the most consistent findings was the need for more training or, in some cases, even initial instruction to accompany the drills that were being conducted. Teachers across multiple studies have indicated that more training and drills are needed to improve preparedness efforts; furthermore, educators have noted that variation is needed in the scenarios being practiced. Alternating the delivery methods of training also was highlighted by some teachers as a way to keep the content fresh and relevant. Similarly, training with first responders and other community agencies was noted by teachers as an important part of the preparedness efforts. Training with first responders can help educators become more familiar with what to expect in the event of an actual emergency, which in turn can potentially reduce anxieties that may arise as a result of the stress of the event and corresponding response.

In addition to training in the schools' emergency preparedness protocols, educators have highlighted the need for guidance on other practices that may be relevant. Emergency care training, such as CPR, first aid, and basic life support, has been highlighted by teachers as an essential area in which they should receive instruction.[17] This is particularly important because school personnel may have to assume the role of first responders in the immediate aftermath of crisis events that occur at a school.[18] Such training can be used to respond not only in active shooter situations but also in other emergencies that school personnel may encounter in which lifesaving skills are needed. Another form of emergency care referenced by teachers is Stop the Bleed training. Stop the Bleed is a national campaign designed by the Department of Homeland

Table 6.1 Staff perceptions of improvements needed related to training and drills

- Ensure that all building-level employees (administration, staff, and faculty, including substitutes) have the necessary initial training.
- Provide additional or ongoing training and drills to practice for different scenarios.
- Vary timing of training (e.g., not only at the start of the school year) to ensure it can be accessed by all who need it.
- Require an annual review of written emergency operations plan and associated training.
- Provide guidance and training on other relevant practices, including, but not limited to, CPR, first aid, basic life support, and Stop the Bleed.
- Offer opportunities to train with first responders and other community agencies to improve coordination and develop an understanding of what may happen during a real emergency.
- Ensure consistency of practices and procedures within and between schools and districts.
- Prioritize drills and training as more than "tick-box exercises."

Sources: Bethney Bergh, "A Qualitative Study of School Lockdown Procedures and Teachers' Ability to Conduct and Implement them at the Classroom Level," PhD diss., Western Michigan University, 2009; Travis D. Embry-Martin, "Perceptions in Preparing for and Responding to an Active Shooter Incident: A Qualitative Study of K–12 Teachers' Self-Efficacy," PhD diss., Northcentral University, 2017; Jane C. Perkins, "Preparing Teachers for School Tragedy: Reading, Writing, and Lockdown," *Journal of Higher Education Theory and Practice* 18, no. 1 (2018): 70–81, http://m.www.na-businesspress.com/JHETP/JHETP18-1/PerkinsJC_18_1.pdf; Carole Frances Rider, "Teachers' Perceptions of Their Ability to Respond to Active Shooter Incidents," PhD diss., University of Southern Mississippi, 2015; Jaclyn Schildkraut, Amanda B. Nickerson, and Kirsten R. Klingaman, "Reading, Writing, Responding: Educators' Perceptions of Safety, Preparedness, and Lockdown Drills," *Educational Policy* (2021), https://doi.org/10.1177/08959048211015617.

Security to teach members of the general public hemorrhage control in order to save lives.[19] Since individuals with extreme injuries can bleed out in as little as five minutes, the program teaches the proper application of tourniquets to help stabilize wounded individuals until paramedics arrive on scene and can transport them to the hospital for more extensive care. Research on Stop the Bleed programs has shown promise: participants who have gone through the training not only show a greater willingness to intervene in a crisis but also improved knowledge of bleeding control techniques and a willingness to teach the practice to others.[20]

Another critical area for improvement highlighted in studies of teachers' perceptions of lockdown drills is the need for consistency in procedures as well as practices. Several studies found that response practices varied within school districts, particularly among different grade levels. One study in Rhode Island, for example, found that while the schools represented by the 307 respondents all had a generally low rate of implementing different types of drills, such practices occurred more frequently at the elementary schools compared to the middle and high schools.[21] Maintaining consistency both in the protocols and in how they are practiced is important for several reasons. First, educators as well as students can move between schools in a given district, so having consistency in procedures ensures they will know how to respond if faced with an emergency no matter what building they are in, without having to retrain in a different protocol. Second, having uniformity across schools in a district leads to greater predictability not only for internal safety teams but for first responders as well. While protocols may be standardized, it is vital that training and practice be conducted on individuals' primary campuses to ensure their familiarity with the environments, which can play a critical role in emergency response.

Educators have identified several other important considerations related to lockdown drills and emergency preparedness. Since the majority of schools have written emergency response or crisis plans for active shooter events,[22] educators should be encouraged to review these plans annually or more frequently. Initial formal training and annual refreshers similarly should be provided for all preparedness practices to ensure a continued familiarity with expectations of how to respond in emergencies. In light of the high turnover rate in school faculty, paired with the number of substitute teachers who may be active in a district on any given day, training options must also be provided to ensure that *all* educators working in the building have the necessary skills and tools, such as keys, to respond if an emergency were to occur while they were there. In other words, training cannot be restricted to the beginning of the academic year but should occur at intervals throughout the school year, and schools should have in place alternative delivery methods to provide the information on an ongoing basis as needed. Drills and training sessions must be prioritized and not passed over because of scheduling conflicts.

BUILDING NOT ONLY COOPERATION AND COLLABORATION BUT ALSO CONFIDENCE

News stories have recounted the experiences of educators who have participated in "drills gone wrong"—those that make headlines for being particularly extreme or leading to some type of horrific outcome. In April 2013, for example, an Oregon elementary school teacher participated in a simulated school shooting during which the perpetrator, a role filled by the school's safety supervisor, pointed a prop gun at her face, pulled the trigger, and told her she was dead.[23] Never told it was a drill, the teacher subsequently was diagnosed with posttraumatic stress disorder (PTSD) and was unable to return to the school after. In March 2019, elementary school teachers in Indiana were shot execution style with pellet guns by trainers, ultimately sustaining both physical and emotional injuries.[24] In both instances, lawsuits were filed. Not all drills are equal, and most do not rise to the level of these teachers' experiences, but the manner in which drills are conducted can have significant implications for educators' emotional well-being, as well as their perceived safety and preparedness.

Educators who perceive themselves to be safe at school may be able to more successfully manage their own potentially adverse reactions to lockdown drills. Perceiving their schools as being safe institutions can reinforce the idea that lockdown drills are a routine practice rather than an indicator of an imminent, serious event, such as a shooting threat. A study of K–12 teachers' perceptions of school-based policies (which focused on more punitive measures such as suspension or expulsion rather than on lockdown drills), for example, found that fear of school violence can be abated when said policies are perceived to be effective,[25] and this effect may similarly extend to emergency preparedness training. Best practices highlight the importance of educators modeling calm behavior for students as a tool to help mitigate the potential trauma that can arise from participating in lockdown drills or even in real-world active shooter events.[26] As the research findings discussed here suggest, it is possible to foster a culture of preparedness among school faculty, staff, and administrators. When individuals perceive themselves as being better equipped to respond in an emergency, they may also feel more comfortable doing so.

Even more broadly, improving perceptions of school safety and preparedness can have important benefits for educators, including increasing their work engagement.[27] Stress and burnout, to which this group is particularly prone, also may be mitigated.[28] These considerations, taken together, present important implications for students relative to their learning and overall success, as well as their educational environment. Further, while teachers, school staff, and administrators are charged with ensuring students get an education, they also are tasked with helping prepare them for emergencies. Ensuring they have the proper skills available to carry out this task is critical.

Although taking steps to prepare for active shooter events, a threat that is statistically rare yet one that schools must be ready for, may invoke fear among educators, having the necessary training and practice to be able to do so actually can potentially mitigate this, at least in part. Yet it is not sufficient simply to have a plan. That plan must be practiced, assessed, and revised as necessary to further foster a culture of preparedness. In the next chapter, we examine research that explores the procedural integrity of drills: that is, how well they are conducted relative to the required steps. Witnessing or participating in practices that are carried out correctly can have positive impacts on perceived safety and preparedness on the part of educators and students alike.

7

TEACHING THE STEPS OF LOCKDOWN
MORE THAN JUST DRILLING

Key Takeaways

- Evaluating drills is important for understanding whether response procedures and plans are being practiced correctly.
- Drills can be evaluated in different ways, all of which provide opportunities to offer feedback for improving future practices.
- Research has found that skill mastery with students is possible with continued practice and drills.
- Combining drills with training helps improve not only skill mastery but also buy-in from participants as they are better able to understand why they are performing each step.

Understanding the effects of lockdown drills on perceived safety and preparedness, as well as on other aspects, such as anxiety, is critical when evaluating the impacts of such practices. There are other considerations, however, that must be factored into such assessments. If a primary goal of drills is to build muscle memory so that individuals can respond as needed in times of crisis when their cognitive processing may be impaired, such as from stress,[1] then evaluating the relationship between such practices and skill mastery (or the procedural integrity of the drill overall) is warranted. Without such information, schools are engaging in practices without knowing whether they work, which may in turn result in such efforts potentially leading to more harm than good.

The manner in which such practices are conducted runs the gamut, from simple tabletop exercises to the traditional drills most often conducted in schools. Variation in how these practices are conducted can lead to differences in assessments of them.[2] In this chapter, we examine research findings that consider skill acquisition related to conducting drills. We also explore the potential benefits of including training in emergency preparedness efforts as a way to bolster the procedural integrity of the drills.

WHY EVALUATING DRILLS IS NECESSARY

At an individual level, drills are important because they are designed to teach people self-protective behaviors that can be used in emergencies to reduce both fatal and nonfatal injuries.[3] Drills conducted regularly and in accordance with best practices increase the likelihood that, in an actual emergency, individuals will respond in a predictable manner using situation-specific tactics.[4] Conversely, drills that are poorly designed or executed can result in deficient performance in a crisis, meaning that people may not respond in the manner that is most appropriate for the situation. They also can exacerbate fears over a threat, create a false sense of security, and minimize confidence in preparedness efforts.[5]

At an administrative level, drills are important because they help validate response plans and procedures. Drills may be viewed by participants as an inconvenience to their daily schedule or as tick-box exercises with little meaning.[6] Yet for those tasked with ensuring the safety and security of everyone in the building, drills provide a template for assessing the potential response during an actual emergency. Evaluating drills therefore provides an opportunity to verify that the goals or objectives of the procedure are being met, which can help ensure that preparedness efforts are as effective as possible.[7] Such evaluation also provides an opportunity to collect feedback, which is necessary for improving plans and protocols. Since the types of emergency scenarios for which schools and other organizations must prepare are constantly evolving, evaluating drills can identify ways in which emergency plans should be adapted to meet these changing needs.

Drill evaluation can take place in a number of different ways.[8] Administrators may monitor the practice and generate written after-action reports, or they may consult outside observers. Feedback may be solicited from participants through anonymous evaluations and through discussions in staff meetings or with students in their classrooms. Debriefing with participants can be conducted to assess the strengths and weaknesses of the drill and to identify opportunities for improvement in future practices.

While the majority of schools in the United States conduct lockdown drills, research has indicated there is little corresponding evaluation of these preparedness activities.[9] In many instances, schools may be required to report to their respective state's education department that the drill has been conducted, but the actual quality of the drill goes unassessed. Guidance from both the US Department of Education and the Federal Emergency Management Agency (FEMA) suggests that agencies at the local and federal levels should be involved in drills and emergency preparedness practices to help monitor both the frequency and the quality of drills, but there is no actual enforcement to ensure this oversight is put in place.[10] As a result, not only are drills conducted inconsistently, but variation in the evaluation and assessment of these practices can exaggerate these differences.

RESEARCH EVALUATING DRILL QUALITY

Although there is an emerging body of research examining the perceptions of individuals who participate in lockdown drills, few of these studies are conducted in conjunction with actual drills to assess how taking part in the practice may affect such attitudes. Similarly, few studies have focused on evaluating the procedural integrity of the drills themselves. *Procedural integrity* refers to the number of steps that are correctly carried out to assess whether the response strategy is being executed effectively. Conducting drills allows both researchers and school-level stakeholders—administrators, faculty, staff, and students—to identify not only what steps are done correctly but where adjustments need to be made to increase the quality of the response.

The first research to assess the procedural integrity of a lockdown drill was conducted with a sample of seventy-four students in an elementary school as part of a study examining the impact of such practices on children's anxiety and perceptions of school safety.[11] In preparation for the drill, verbal, cognitive, and behavioral techniques were used with the students: they were provided with the rationale for the drill and for the particular actions being taken, told what specific steps were to be taken, and then observed each step being modeled; they then were able to practice the steps and receive feedback from the group leader before the official practice occurred. Modeling skills is particularly important as it shows students, even those in the youngest age groups, how steps should be performed correctly so that the students can reproduce them in their own actions. During the actual drill, all participants successfully moved to a safe location in the classroom out of sight of the corridor window and were able to do so in under one minute. They were less successful in remaining quiet during the practice, which took approximately seven minutes from initiation to conclusion. Despite the students not successfully remaining quiet for the full length of the drill, the overall noise level did decrease as the practice progressed. The researchers concluded that the drill helped students acquire short-term knowledge about the associated procedures, which can improve their ability to respond in an actual emergency, but that follow-up lessons and practice would be appropriate to help students sustain the skills and address issues that arise, such as not maintaining silence.

A separate study conducted with thirty-two kindergarten students also assessed skill mastery related to lockdown drills.[12] Behavioral skills training (BST), an approach specifically designed to teach safety tactics to children, was used approximately ten minutes before each drill, during which time students were similarly told what the procedures for the practice were, shown how to do them, given the opportunity to rehearse them, and provided with feedback. They then participated in the actual drill, with researchers assessing whether skill mastery, defined as correctly completing six of the seven steps of the practice, was achieved. This assessment, BST plus drill (though feedback was not provided during the latter), was repeated two to three times per week until the students were able to achieve skill mastery for two consecutive sessions. The researchers found that skill mastery was achieved in seven sessions. As in the first study, students exhibited difficulty remaining silent for the duration of the drill, which lasted five minutes. Noise levels did decrease across sessions, however, even with mastery of the step not being fully achieved.

A larger scale study involving thirty K–12 schools in a single district also considered whether continued practice, as well as the introduction of training, had an impact on the procedural integrity of lockdown drills.[13] Two lockdown drills were conducted in each building, one before any training was conducted and one after all schools had received instruction in a new emergency preparedness plan that was being implemented in the district. During each drill, all rooms in the schools were checked for four criteria: (1) whether doors were locked, (2) whether lights were off, (3) whether occupants were out of sight, meaning that they could not be seen or heard from the hallway, and (4) whether anyone in the room responded to the research team knocking on the door, which was designed to simulate someone gaining access to the room. The results of each drill were assessed both individually and comparatively, with the latter analysis designed to determine what impact, if any, the training had on the procedural integrity of the practices.

Before any formal instruction was given in how to respond during a lockdown (drill 1), nearly 87 percent of the rooms that were occupied had their doors locked, though a lesser proportion had their lights off (57 percent) and people out of sight (54 percent). Additionally, when the researchers knocked on the room doors, they received responses nearly 35 percent of the time. After delivery of the training, which was conducted in assembly-style sessions for faculty, staff, and students at the schools, these same criteria were assessed during a follow-up practice (drill 2). While the proportion of doors locked across the district did not change significantly (as it already had been quite high), measurable improvements were found across the three additional criteria being assessed. The proportion of rooms having perfect checks, meaning that they successfully completed all four steps, also nearly doubled between the two drills, as presented in figure 7.1. Following the introduction of training, more rooms completed more steps correctly in the drill process.

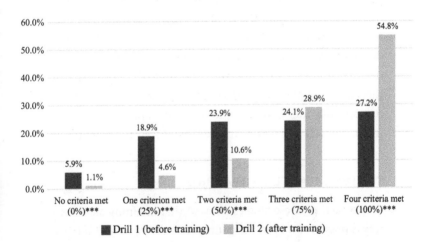

7.1 Procedural integrity of lockdown drills conducted pre- and post-training. *Note.* Three asterisks (***) represents a statistically significant difference between the two drills.

Being able to assess the procedural integrity based on the school level (elementary, middle, combined pre-K to eight, or high school) also allowed the researchers to highlight important opportunities for improvement. For example, a common practice in schools, as was the case in this district, is for building safety teams who are conducting the audit of the drill to also be responsible for securing the room doors from the hallway while they carry out their checks. In a real emergency, however, it is unlikely that key holders would be able to get to rooms without encountering danger; therefore, rooms need to be able to respond and complete all steps of the procedure on their own. When the drill statistics were examined by school level, it was determined that in the elementary schools, the proportion of rooms with their doors locked decreased from the first drill to the second when the administrators were asked not to go out ahead of the research team. This suggested that the teachers had come to rely on administrators to lock their doors and had moved on to other steps in the drill, namely, turning off the lights and getting the students out of sight of the corridor windows (improvements were noted on both metrics after training), and provided an important opportunity to address and correct the behavior for future practices.

THE IMPORTANCE OF TRAINING

While each of these studies showed that attaining skill mastery is possible for even the youngest students, they also highlight an important component of the process that easily can be missed—training. Though drills, including those for lockdowns, provide an important opportunity to assess performance and identify areas in need of improvement, they are not designed to simultaneously act as training. Instead, training and assessment should be treated as two separate parts of a full process to achieve the maximum impact. There may be little value in participating in drills without training because the knowledge, resources, and skills necessary to respond appropriately in a crisis may be missing.[14] Participants also may fail to take the practice as seriously as they would if they were trained, which may affect legitimate skill mastery as participants just "go through the motions" to complete the drill. Therefore, drills and training should not be stand-alone practices—a combination of the two will yield the greatest results related to emergency response.[15]

A key benefit of incorporating training into emergency preparedness programs is that it affords the opportunity to inform participants why they are asked to engage in certain actions, which can lead to greater compliance with key directives during the drill. For example, explaining to students the importance of remaining quiet during the drill—not wanting to let the "bad guy" (perpetrator) know where they are by not calling attention to their room—may increase the likelihood that students comply during the practice. Reminding individuals of the benefit of having the lights off—to have an added layer of concealment—also may ensure that this crucial step is not missed. Since drills are preparation for real-world crises, the effects of such emergencies can be mitigated when people are informed and understand what their responsibilities are in such situations, which increases their buy-in to the procedure.[16] A supplementary benefit of training programs is that individuals may form more realistic judgments of their risk perception relative to a specific type of crisis, such as how likely they think a crisis is to happen versus how likely it is to actually occur.[17]

Training can be conducted in a number of different ways. Previous research evaluating the impact of the introduction of training on the procedural integrity of lockdown drills has focused on an assembly-style delivery. In addition to being both cost- and time-effective by allowing more people to be trained with fewer sessions, assembly-style training enables individuals in different school roles—faculty, staff, student—to receive instruction together, which improves understanding not only of their responsibilities but also of the duties of others so that they know what to expect during a real emergency. In a classroom setting, for example, only teachers would have access to the key necessary to lock the door, thus making that step their responsibility; they also will likely be the one to turn off the lights. By understanding that these tasks are to be completed by the teacher, students know their immediate actions should be getting to the safe location in the room and maintaining silence, with their teacher joining them after the first two steps are completed. Since students need not wait for instructions from their teacher, response time is sped up, which puts precious seconds in their column. Further, since emergency response is not one single person's responsibility, training together can help improve cooperation and coordination during an actual crisis.

Other modalities may also be used to deliver training. Classroom instruction with teachers, which can include lectures and discussion, has been used to help prepare students in their own spaces.[18] Workshops may be paired with classroom instruction to ensure that educators have the materials and information they need to effectively deliver the lessons to their students,[19] as may web-based modules and in-service training.[20] Systems that combine multiple forms of media, such as text, graphics, and sound effects, also known as "hypermedia systems," similarly may be used for training purposes.[21] Interactive computer games have been found by researchers to enhance learning about emergency response strategies,[22] while virtual reality technologies can be used to improve equitability in experiences for students with disabilities who may not be able to fully participate in traditional drills.[23]

It bears noting that in the context of lockdown drills, just a few of these different training techniques have been tried, and none has been directly evaluated for knowledge acquisition and retention. As such, schools should research and subsequently assess any modalities they use to ensure that the goal of effectively delivering training lessons is met. In light of the variability in learning styles and abilities of students, faculty, and staff alike, schools should consider a multipronged approach to ensure that all needs are met.

IMPROVING EVALUATION AND OVERSIGHT

Drills and training are critical to ensure that schools and those within them are prepared for emergencies or disasters that can occur during the daily routine. Yet drills and training are just part of a broader process, and their value increases as the process is better understood. Specifically, schools must first determine what the larger goals of any initiative are. These goals then are used to identify specific objectives needed to meet them, including which scenarios schools need to be prepared for, the type of practice that is best suited to achieve the outcome, and what resources may be needed. Before any practice takes place, planning must occur during which scenarios are crafted (including drill language and debriefing materials), roles are assigned (e.g., identifying who is responsible for checking certain areas of the building and the specific tasks in the process), and a talk-through of the full plan is completed.

Evaluation is an equally critical component of the emergency preparedness process. During drills, tracking forms can be used to increase the accountability of participants by identifying steps that were and were not completed correctly. The use of standardized, structured criteria for such evaluations removes subjective interpretations and increases the likelihood that the data collected are both valid and reliable. Feedback can be provided immediately after the drill during a debriefing session, but these data also can be used to create after-action reports and to develop plans designed to address any areas in need of improvement. Failure to implement changes in response to issues identified during the evaluation process equates to missed opportunities to improve the safety and well-being of those involved. At the same time, just making changes is not sufficient. Once these potential improvements are implemented, additional drills must be conducted to ensure that they address the issues they were designed to address and that the issue has been corrected. To be as effective as possible, both training and drills ultimately should be informed by best practices, which we review in the next chapter.

POLICY AND BEST PRACTICES

III

POLICY AND BEST PRACTICES

8

HOW SHOULD WE THINK ABOUT LOCKDOWN DRILLS?
GUIDANCE AND BEST PRACTICES

Key Takeaways

- Best practices in planning, conducting, and evaluating drills have been identified by organizations and researchers.
- Before lockdown drills are conducted, a multidisciplinary safety team should engage in careful planning, making sure that the plan takes into account students and staff with disabilities or other specific needs, and should provide training.
- Drills should be announced, so that they are not confused with an actual crisis, and should be conducted at different times and on different days.
- A trauma-informed approach should be used to plan for, identify, and respond to potential distress arising from participating in drills.
- Drills should be evaluated for procedural integrity and impact (including traumatic reactions), and the information should be used to improve future practice.

Although there is a critical need for continued research and national standards for lockdown drills, these efforts likely will take more time to develop than schools and communities can afford to wait. Lockdown drills are being conducted across the country on a routine basis, with considerable disparity in practices. Fortunately, several federal agencies, national and state organizations, and researchers have identified and circulated best practices for planning, conducting, and evaluating drills. These recommended practices are designed to maximize drills' effectiveness in teaching and practicing skills, improving muscle memory, and preparing schools to respond while incorporating strategies to help mitigate potential harm to participants.

In this chapter, we explore best practices relative to conducting lockdown drills. We highlight the need for multidisciplinary safety teams to engage in careful planning to progress from discussion-based training to more complex exercises, and to provide guidance for training as it relates to developmentally appropriate practices and considerations for students and staff with disabilities and other specific needs. Recognizing the importance of vulnerable populations and the need to attend to social-emotional reactions, we describe a trauma-informed approach to conducting lockdown drills. The need to prepare and practice for a variety of threats and hazards is emphasized, as is the evaluation of the effectiveness, integrity, and impact of drills. Table 8.1 highlights some key best practice considerations to be observed before, during, and after conducting drills, each of which then is described in greater detail, with selected resources and examples.

ESTABLISH A MULTIDISCIPLINARY SAFETY TEAM

As recommended by the US Department of Education and numerous other education-focused organizations, a core

Table 8.1 Best practices before, during, and after lockdown drills

Timeframe	Recommended Practice
Before	• Establish a multidisciplinary safety team. • Engage in careful planning. ◦ Practice multiple response protocols to prepare for all threats and hazards. ◦ Use a progressive approach that weighs costs and benefits. • Plan for students and staff with disabilities and other specific needs. • Be clear about drill objective and terminology. • Provide training for all school staff and students. ◦ Include full- and part-time staff, substitutes, and volunteers. ◦ Use developmentally appropriate practices. ◦ Provide specialized training and practice for students with disabilities.
During	• Use a trauma-informed approach. • Conduct drills at varying times of the day and on different days. • Announce the drill.
After	• Evaluate. ◦ Assess procedural integrity. ◦ Assess impact (including assessing and responding to potential traumatic reactions). ◦ Determine improvements needed.

multidisciplinary safety team should include administrators, educators, school-based mental health professionals (psychologists, counselors, social workers), and nurses, as well as representatives from facilities, transportation, and food services.[1] The team also should include student and parent representatives, community partners (including law enforcement), emergency medical services, fire officials, public and mental health practitioners, and organizations that serve and represent students, staff, and parents with disabilities and other diverse needs (e.g., those relating to language, religion, and racial and ethnic diversity). The American Academy of Pediatrics' Policy Statement further recommends including professionals with expertise in child development and behavioral health, such as pediatricians and school-based mental health providers, to evaluate students' emotional reactions and the impact of drills.[2]

ENGAGE IN CAREFUL PLANNING

The multidisciplinary safety team should engage in planning through a careful and deliberative process. The team must consult relevant state laws and local requirements and consider all threats and hazards, using assessment data to consider the school's unique needs and resources. The best practice is to have school staff and students drill in multiple protocols, including lockdown, secure (also known as lockout), evacuate, hold in place, and shelter in place, so that they are prepared to take specific, appropriate actions in response to a wide variety of threats and hazards. Drills are most useful when they are based on data relative to the school's vulnerabilities, such as location and population, to prepare individuals for the types of threats and hazards that are most probable. It also is recommended that school districts have a memorandum of understanding (MOU) with local emergency response organizations. Careful planning should utilize a progressive approach, moving from simple, low-cost, discussion-based exercises to more complex options-based exercises.

PLAN FOR STUDENTS AND STAFF WITH DISABILITIES AND OTHER SPECIFIC NEEDS

Planning must take into account the access and functional needs of the whole school community. School safety teams should consult a disability specialist when planning drills. Accommodations for disabilities that are physical, sensory, or cognitive in nature also should be incorporated into the plan as these disabilities may impede understanding or response to instruction during the drill or in an actual emergency. When creating emergency plans, schools should consult special education teachers, families, and the students themselves, if appropriate, to identify what accommodations are needed and include this information on a roster of students with disabilities or special needs that it maintains. At annual Individualized Education Program (IEP) meetings for students in special education programs, the team should ask whether there is a specific plan for the student's individual needs in the event of a crisis or emergency.[3] Accommodations or Individual Emergency and Lockdown Plans (IELP)[4] can be part of a student's 504 Plan or IEP.[5] This plan should be shared with all teachers and other support personnel who work with the student, and copies also should be provided to the student, such as in a backpack, planner, or tablet. Teachers and others who work with students with disabilities should be instructed as to their specific role in supporting and accommodating the students during the emergencies.

Information to be included in the IELP should include student strengths relevant to emergency situations (e.g., follows directions from an adult); medical, communication, and sensory needs; other critical information (e.g., agitated by loud noises); and what should be included in an emergency kit. For example, students who seek tactile pressure and who may have difficulty remaining quiet or staying still could be provided with sensory toys such as stress balls, markers, or stretchy string and snacks to occupy them during a lockdown drill. It also is important for schools to accommodate students whose first language is not English by providing announcements or instructions in their native language.[6] Additionally, students and staff with other communication difficulties may need different signals to indicate lockdown, such as lighting alerts on an alternative communication system or a vibrating pager.

BE CLEAR ABOUT DRILL OBJECTIVES AND TERMINOLOGY

When planning for drills, it is important to be clear about the learning objectives for the participants.[7] Drills focus on teaching and practicing skills and improving muscle memory with members of the entire school community. This can be achieved without simulating actual crisis events or the use of stage blood or sounds of gunfire, which are considered high intensity and unnecessary for achieving these goals.[8] Full-scale exercises, in contrast, primarily serve to test the capacity and training of law enforcement.[9] If full-scale exercises are to be employed, schools should be informed of this purpose and only volunteers should participate. If high-intensity live exercises are involved, potential participants should be fully informed of what will take place, their role, and the possible distress that may result from the experience.

With this information, adult participants, including school staff or the parents of children, can give informed consent, and children of appropriate age and developmental level can agree to participate or opt out.[10]

It is important to clearly differentiate among the various types of drills and to use clear and consistent terminology. For example, the phrase "active shooter drill" can be problematic when used as a catch-all phrase to refer to a range of practices that may include lockdowns, options-based approaches, and full-scale exercises. It is important to strive for clarity and to use standardized language, as the use of codes (e.g., "Code Red") can be confusing. Standardized language is important so that it is clear to educators, students, parents, first responders, and community members what actions are about to be performed.

PROVIDE TRAINING

It is essential that training be provided to all individuals who are routinely in the building, including full- and part-time teaching staff, support staff, administrators, volunteers, contractors, substitute teachers, and students, so that they know what to do if a lockdown is announced.[11] Training also improves participants' understanding of why the drills are important, which can increase compliance and buy-in. To coordinate lockdowns and other drills as part of safety planning, it is highly recommended that members of both district and school-based safety teams complete the Federal Emergency Management Agency (FEMA) training on the National Incident Management System (NIMS), the Incident Command

System, and review planning for multiple hazards and threats. These training opportunities are offered as free online courses through FEMA's Emergency Management Institute at https://training.fema.gov/nims.

Educators and students should be trained in multiple response protocols in addition to lockdowns so that they are prepared to take action in response to the different threats and hazards the school may encounter. When training is to be conducted, several scenarios should be discussed, and it should be emphasized to participants that they need to listen for instructions, as protocols may follow one another rapidly in response to emerging events. For example, a lockdown might be called when there is an intruder in a building, but once police have secured the scene, the school may transition into an evacuation to a reunification site. Individuals should be trained in how to proceed if they are in hallways, cafeterias, or other open areas, emphasizing that securing themselves behind the closest locked door is the best strategy but that if this is not possible, they should evacuate to safety. During the training session, the multiple access points—windows, fire escape, outside door, main door—in a room should be reviewed to ensure that individuals understand that all of these must be locked and secured. A specific safe zone where everyone in the room can stay out of sight in a lockdown should be designated, and it may be helpful to mark this area with tape. During the training session, people should also be advised that a lockdown may last several hours. For this and other reasons, classrooms should be equipped with emergency "go kits" with vital supplies, including, for example, water, snacks, an attendance roster, emergency contact information, a communication device, and medications.

The training session should allow the opportunity for participants to ask questions. Table 8.2 lists some common questions and answers regarding lockdown drills. There may be questions about these procedures, particularly if they have changed over time or if students or staff have moved from another state or area. Although there are standard protocols, different jurisdictions advise schools differently on some aspects, such as whether or not to close the blinds or turn the lights off, so it is important that schools work in collaboration with their local emergency responders and involve them in the training. It also is common for people to ask "What if . . . ?" scenarios. For example, people may want more guidance on what to do in the extremely rare event that they come face-to-face with an armed assailant. Participants can be advised that safety is the priority and that how they choose to respond if confronted by an active shooter is up to that person and situation. Training should not be a one-time event; rather, it is recommended that schools provide frequent updates and refresher training sessions annually.[12] Posters can also be provided to hang in classrooms, cafeterias, hallways, and other areas in the school as reminders of the protocols. Figure 8.1 shows such a poster reminding students and staff of the procedures for hold, secure, lockdown, evacuate, and shelter.

USE DEVELOPMENTALLY APPROPRIATE TRAINING AND DRILL PRACTICES

Schools must be mindful of the developmental level of awareness of their students, which has practical implications for how the training and lockdown drills are conducted.[13] At the preschool and early elementary levels, children demonstrate

Table 8.2 Sample questions and answers about lockdown drills

Question: Why do we do lockdown drills?
Answer: We do lockdown drills to make sure that you know what to do in case there is an emergency in the building, such as a wild animal or an intruder with a gun. Just as we practice in case there is a fire, this is something we practice to keep ourselves safe.
Question: What if I am in the bathroom when the drill is called?
Answer: If you are in a bathroom, stay there. Close the lock on the main bathroom door if there is one. If not, lock yourself in a stall and sit on the toilet with your feet up so no one can see you. Remain still and quiet.
Question: If I am in the hallway and the teacher locks the door, what do I do?
Answer: If the teacher locks the door and you cannot get in, try the next closest room. If that also is locked, do what you can to get out of the building and away to safety.
Question: What do we do if we are outside when the lockdown is called?
Answer: Stay outside and move as far away from the building as possible (go to the school's reunification point or notify the school district if you go somewhere else). A lockdown is called when the threat is inside the building, so you do not want to come back inside the building.
Question: In my last school, we had to close the blinds on the window, but here we do not. Why?
Answer: We follow the guidance of our local police, who say that the best practice is to leave windows uncovered so that they can see inside the room when they come to help. Since the standard practice is to leave windows uncovered, having blinds closed or windows covered could signal that someone in the room covered them.
Question: Is being quiet important?
Answer: Yes! If people in the room are quiet, someone outside will think that the room is empty if they cannot see anyone. Making noise draws attention to the room.
Question: What can be done if a shooter gets into the classroom?
Answer: If a shooter gets into the classroom, do whatever you have to. Run out of the room and as far away as possible if you can. Throw things to distract them. The situation will dictate what you can do, but the most important thing is get to safety as fast as possible.

8.1 Sample poster from the Standard Response Protocol. *Source:* "I Love U Guys" Foundation, "The Standard Response Protocol K–12" (2021).

a basic understanding of "danger" but still require adult guidance in distinguishing probable from all possible threats, as
well as in determining what is unsafe and what is not. At this
age, students often are taught about safety skills in potentially dangerous situations (e.g., holding hands while crossing
a street, not going into the water without an adult present,
staying away from a hot stove). When explaining safety-based
activities, it is best to use concrete examples to explain common dangers that adults may address. It also is recommended
to use the term "safety drill" when describing the process and
to compare the lockdown practice to fire drills. During emergency situations, children in this age group are heavily depen-
dent on adult management and direction, yet they are able
to understand and follow basic safety directions such as "Get
out," "Evacuate," or "Hide out."

At the upper elementary level, children have more knowledge about what is dangerous and what is not, but still may
require some adult guidance. These students can understand
why drills are conducted and can understand all safety directions and instructions. When explaining safety-based activities to this age group, it is best to use common examples.
For instance, they can be reminded that they wear a helmet
when riding a bike or a seat belt in the car to keep them safe.
It also is recommended to teach the difference between rare
and common dangers (car accidents are more common than
shootings in schools), as this age group still may struggle
with differentiating between the two.

Middle school–aged students generally have all the skills
previously learned and are able to distinguish probable from
possible dangers without adult guidance. When teaching about

safety-based activities, it is helpful to engage in discussions with the students and allow them to generate examples of common dangers that may occur in the school. During emergencies, students at this level may still benefit from teacher direction but are able to perform practiced actions independently.

High school students, adults, and volunteers in the school are likely to understand a range of emergency safety actions and able to match the appropriate response strategies to specific scenarios. When teaching about safety-based activities, it is beneficial to engage in discussions with the students regarding the need for and types of safety-based plans. During emergencies, high school students still may benefit from adult direction but are able to independently perform practiced actions and adapt protocols to the situation.

PROVIDE STUDENTS WITH DISABILITIES OPPORTUNITIES FOR SPECIALIZED TRAINING AND PRACTICE

Students with disabilities may need more frequent training and practice in lockdown drills. This training involves ensuring that students understand what the crisis plan is and why it is needed, as well as how to communicate with first responders if possible.[14] Training therefore may include teaching them to recognize emergency personnel uniforms and badges and having them meet and practice with emergency responders. Educators have developed various social stories to guide students through lockdown procedures (see teacherspayteachers .com and search for the term "lockdown drills"). Other students may benefit from a picture schedule that visually depicts each step of a lockdown drill and from a reinforcement plan that includes receiving rewards for following directions after a specified period of time.[15]

USE A TRAUMA-INFORMED APPROACH

Individuals with anxiety disorders, previous traumatic experiences, or other vulnerabilities also need to be considered when planning for and conducting lockdown drills.[16] It is important to know the histories of students and educators in the school and to train school-based personnel to recognize trauma and stress reactions, model calm responses, and proactively plan for preventing and addressing potential distress and anxiety. For individuals showing signs of anxiety or who may have preexisting vulnerabilities, utilizing coping strategies is recommended. These strategies can include pairing them with a trusted peer or adult, using stabilization and grounding techniques (e.g., deep breathing; naming nondistressing sights, sounds, or objects), and praising students for specific actions they took to care for themselves or others. Since educators may not know the trauma histories of students or the extent to which the drills can trigger anxiety or other traumatic responses, however, the use of calming techniques may be of benefit for all students.

A school-based mental health professional such as a psychologist or counselor should be present during lockdown drills. In one example, a school psychologist identified two students with trauma histories related to guns and incorporated a trauma-informed approach when planning the building's drill. The students went into lockdown with their respective school counselors to provide a sense of comfort and safety. They also were able to debrief with the counselor immediately after the drill.[17] It is highly recommended that an identified staff member check in with students with known trauma histories after the drill and provide mental health referrals for students who still are struggling a week or more after the drill. Beyond individuals with vulnerabilities, it is a good practice for teachers and school staff to debrief with one another and for parents to talk with their children after the drill. Teachers and parents also can be advised of signs to look for in the days and weeks following the drill that may signal that a child is experiencing difficulties from drill participation; some of these signs are the child frequently asking "what if" questions regarding school shootings or exhibiting a startle response to loud noises. Teachers, parents, and students themselves should be encouraged to speak with a school-based mental health professional, such as a counselor, psychologist, or social worker, if they have concerns following the drill.

CONDUCT DRILLS AT VARYING TIMES OF THE DAY AND ON DIFFERENT DAYS

Although schools may be tempted to conduct drills at a standard time and on a preestablished day for consistency and efficiency, the best practice is to schedule drills variably.[18] Drills provide an opportunity not only to practice skills and improve muscle memory but also to make fast and effective decisions in different circumstances. During the lunch period, for example, students are likely to be in the cafeteria or common areas. Depending on the setup of the school, this situation may present a vulnerability because of the larger number of people, the reduced likelihood of having a lockable door within range to secure behind, and less adult supervision. Drills during this time can be helpful in training all school staff and students in how to respond in these circumstances. They also can be useful in identifying problems, reassessing protocols, and implementing solutions to issues that may arise during these times of increased vulnerability.

Some studies of educators' perceptions of drills have indicated the need for more realistic situations or simulations, so that instead of repeatedly practicing the same procedure, they have the opportunity to run through different responses.[19] This does not mean that highly sensorial or potentially traumatizing props and stimuli are needed. It does, however, mean that different scenarios should be introduced that require participants to adapt their responses. For example, a lockdown drill may transition into a fire drill, threats may be announced in different locations in the building, or obstacles such as a nonlocking door may be included in the drill. Another important time to consider conducting drills is during arrival, dismissal, and class changes, and at times when there are more substitute or part-time staff.[20] Schools also should consider practicing at off-peak times such as during after-school activities (sports practices, club meetings). Finally, lockdown drills and other emergency responses, such as evacuation, may be coupled with other procedures, such as reunification with families, which also should be practiced.

ANNOUNCE THE DRILL

To avoid confusion and increase transparency, clear communication about drills is vital. Information about drills can be communicated in the parent handbook and on the school's website using parent-friendly material. The information should include the types of drills and their frequency or schedule, how parents will be notified about them (e.g., through an emergency alert system, by email), and how the practices will help the school community. Parents also should be notified about their role in the drills, such as whether they are allowed to observe or participate, and should be informed that they may not be permitted to enter the building, pick up their child, or communicate with their child during the practice. Keeping parents informed can minimize the likelihood that they will respond in a detrimental way during an actual emergency.

It is recommended that the school announce to school faculty, staff, students, and parents the general time window, such as a one-week period, in which a drill is to be conducted. While the drill is in progress, signs should be posted on the school lawn and at any entrance where people can access the building notifying staff and visitors that a drill is in progress and that no one may enter or exit the building until the practice is completed. Reminders of the drill can be shared on the school's social media accounts, and a member of the school's crisis team should monitor these platforms during the drill to correct misinformation. Clear notification of the community is particularly important if the drill is to involve law enforcement and other emergency responders, to prevent confusion and rumors from spreading.

The school also should clearly announce that "This is a drill." Drills must not be mistaken for actual crisis events, and schools should not lead anyone to believe that the practice is a real event or that people have been injured or killed. Misleading people to believe that there is a threat to their health or safety is both harmful and unethical. Indeed, it is reports of these practices, where people are deliberately led to believe that there is an active shooter or other threat, that has fueled much of the concern about drills. Schools also must have working emergency notification systems, such as a public announcement system that reaches all rooms in building or devices such as bullhorns or walkie-talkies.[21] If alarms or sirens are to accompany the drills, everyone must be trained in what these signals sound like.[22]

EVALUATE FOR INTEGRITY, IMPACT, AND IMPROVEMENTS

Drills offer an important opportunity to learn from the experience and to make improvements. It has been recommended that schools use an evaluation mindset to inform their crisis response planning, set the expectation that mistakes or inconsistencies during drills are opportunities to improve future crisis responses, and better understand what was done and provide information to be used in making improvements and modify practices.[23] Evaluation can include observation of the drill to assess performance. Assessing procedural integrity, or the number of steps that are performed correctly, and the response time to complete the process also can help achieve this aim. An example of a procedural integrity checklist is provided in figure 8.2. The school safety team also should track the number and types of drills conducted annually.

After a drill, time should be designated to debrief with faculty, staff, administrators, and students. Debriefing provides an opportunity to check for understanding of the drill procedures, to note strengths and weaknesses, and to identify areas

| Date/Time: _____ | School: _____ |
| Location (Room number): _____ | Completion time: _____ |

Name of person completing checklist:_____

Step	Completed?	Notes
Are the doors and all other access points to the room (e.g., windows) locked?	☐ Yes ☐ No	
Are the lights turned off?	☐ Yes ☐ No	
Are all room occupants out of visible sight from the corridor window?	☐ Yes ☐ No	
Are all room occupants maintaining silence (cannot be heard from the hallway)?	☐ Yes ☐ No	
Did the occupants keep the door locked in response to a knock?	☐ Yes ☐ No	

8.2 Lockdown drill procedural integrity checklist. *Source:* Adapted from "I Love U Guys" Foundation (2021), note 1. Guidance for turning the lights off may vary by jurisdiction, so schools should verify the protocol with their local law enforcement.

in need of improvement. It also is important to be attentive to possible unintended emotional consequences of drills, such as increased levels of fear or anxiety, particularly among individuals with preexisting vulnerabilities or trauma histories; school-based mental health professionals should be available to facilitate individual or small-group debriefings for these reactions.

Surveys or feedback forms can be administered to school staff, students, and emergency responders to rate the effectiveness of the drills and perceptions of preparedness, strengths, and areas for improvement, as well as to solicit input about the execution and logistics of the drill. Information from these different sources should be analyzed and incorporated into an after-action report that synthesizes the strengths of the drill, the areas for improvement, and any corrective actions that are needed for future practices.

MOVING FORWARD: ADDITIONAL CONSIDERATIONS FOR RESEARCH, POLICY, AND PRACTICE

Beyond asking those individuals who participate in drills to evaluate them to make ongoing improvements, there is a critical need for researchers to conduct more studies using a variety of methodological approaches to assess the effectiveness of different types of drills and their impacts on skill mastery, perceptions of preparedness, and unintended consequences, such as fear and anxiety. This research should assess not only impact but also the protocol used for the training sessions and drills.[24] This is especially important in light of the great variability in drills and exercises, as having such information can help schools choose the program that is the best fit for their educators and students. Findings from this evaluation and research should be used to help shape policies and practices so that science can inform decision-making.

As emphasized throughout this chapter, decisions about lockdown drills are made by multidisciplinary safety teams within the larger framework of school safety. These drills should not be viewed or implemented as isolated events, add-ons, or items to check off on a list. Rather, if conducted according to the best practices, they can provide meaningful opportunities to teach and practice skills, improve muscle memory, and test and improve plans. In the next chapter, we provide the broader context of school safety and where lockdowns fit within it. We also consider the evidence for lockdown drills in comparison to the proposed solutions for school safety offered by the booming consumer product market.

9

LOCKDOWN DRILLS
A PIECE OF THE SCHOOL SAFETY PUZZLE

Key Takeaways

- Keeping schools safe requires a proactive and layered approach.
- Target-hardening approaches (e.g., increased security and controlled access) are used because schools are especially vulnerable to threats from having large groups of people in largely exposed and unguarded spaces.
- Administrators and policymakers should consider not only the lack of evidence for the effectiveness of visible security measures but also their impacts on the school's climate.
- Schools should be proactive in developing comprehensive safety plans, including those for emergency operations, that cover the five mission areas of the US Department of Education guidance.
- Planning should also consider both the school and its community members (students, staff) to ensure all unique needs are met.

How best to keep schools safe is a question constantly on the minds of educators, administrators, policymakers, parents, and even students. It has become all the more pertinent in the aftermath of high-profile mass shootings in schools, including those at Columbine (1999), Sandy Hook (2012), and Parkland (2018). Such events generate not only fears of violence but also drastic changes in security-related policies and procedures within schools designed to reduce the opportunities for victimization.[1] Lockdown drills and associated procedures were formalized after the Columbine shooting as a way to ensure that students and their educators are prepared to respond if faced with a similar situation. There also was a significant focus on increasing visible security measures to deter future incidents of school violence.[2] Simultaneously, the school security consumer product market produced a "feeding frenzy" that saw expenditures reaching $2.7 billion in 2017, with continued growth each year thereafter.[3] Questions have been raised, however, as to whether all these measures have merely created a false sense of security, insofar as many of the available options lack any evidence of efficacy in keeping schools safe during shootings or other acts of violence.[4]

School safety is a complex, multidimensional issue that requires a layered approach to ensure that all associated aspects are both considered and addressed. To this point, we have argued that lockdown drills and emergency preparedness protocols more broadly are one such layer or piece of the puzzle that must be put in place. Here we consider other possible layers within the bigger picture of school safety, such as the various measures that have been introduced in the wake of Columbine and other shootings. We also explore broader focal points for comprehensive school safety plans recommended by the US Department of Education and where lockdowns fit within them.

A HARDENING APPROACH TO SCHOOL SAFETY

Schools often are referred to as "soft targets" because there is a large concentration of people in an area that is not fortified, ultimately leaving those inside unprotected and vulnerable.[5] Soft targets are attractive to potential perpetrators because they are less likely to encounter resistance when carrying out their attack. As a result, responses to school shootings largely have focused on how to make buildings less vulnerable by hardening or adding security mechanisms. Moreover, schools went to considerable lengths to ensure not only that such systems were in place but also that they were visible.

Following Columbine, schools increased their use of metal detectors and security cameras.[6] It bears noting that these devices were not new to educational buildings but had been concentrated more in urban schools for at least two decades before Columbine in response to both property crimes, such as vandalism and graffiti, and increasing levels of violence. After the shooting, however, there was a general demand to integrate such technologies into suburban and rural schools as well. In the year after Columbine (1999–2000), just 19 percent of schools were utilizing security cameras; by the 2015–2016 academic year, this figure had ballooned to more than 80 percent,[7] in large part owing to the federal funding made available to support the purchase and installation of the technology. Metal detectors are used less frequently in schools, particularly compared to random checks of students, but their use also increased after both Columbine and Sandy Hook, with additional calls for use following Parkland.

Another popular form of target hardening in response to school shootings is controlled building access, which focuses on prevention, or creating a positive security image that deters a potential perpetrator, and mitigation, which typically entails restricting entry, creating time for building occupants to respond.[8] The use of controlled access, often focused on a school's main entrances, draws on the theory of crime prevention through environmental design (CPTED), a concept introduced in the 1970s.[9] This perspective seeks to proactively prevent crime by creating defensible spaces through *territoriality* (creating legitimate ownership of spaces by specific users, such as educators and students, whereby intruders are more easily identifiable), *natural surveillance* (creating the perception that people are being observed, which makes them less likely to engage in crime), and *access control* (limiting the opportunity for offenders to converge with their intended targets). Schools have been able to integrate these features into their buildings in a number of different ways, including but not limited to single-point entries, vestibules and double-entry systems, electronic access control, visitor screening and management programs (through video intercoms, proof of identification, and the issuance of badges), door hardware, and perimeter fencing.

Perhaps the most popular visible measure for schools, particularly in the aftermath of school shootings, is the increased presence of armed security personnel on campus. This included school resource officers (SROs), for which federal funding was made available to help support, as well as law enforcement and private security. The use of SROs began in the early 1950s in Flint, Michigan,[10] but their use largely expanded after Columbine when, in the spring of 2000, President Bill Clinton allocated more than $60 million in funding to support installing 452 security officers in schools through the Community Oriented Policing Services (COPS) office of the US Department of Justice.[11] Between then and 2005, when the COPS in Schools program ended, more than 7,200 positions had been funded to the tune of $823 million.[12] More than $1 billion in funding has been spent specifically on policing in schools, with an additional $14 billion invested into community policing initiatives, which may also include SROs.[13] Since Parkland, armed-teacher policies have gained particular traction as a way to supplement SROs and other security personnel at schools.[14] Approximately five hundred school districts in twenty-eight states permitted armed teachers on campus in some capacity as of January 2020.[15]

Although each of these measures individually and collectively increased visible security within schools, there are three significant challenges to their use. The first issue is the resources, particularly financial, needed not only to initiate any one of these solutions but also to maintain them. The annual cost to employ an SRO ranges from $50,000 to $80,000 per year, meaning that it could cost upward of $11 billion annually to have just one in each of the more than 130,000 public K–12 schools in the United States.[16] Even if funding is obtained through the COPS office, which supports fewer than one thousand positions annually, this covers only 75 percent of an SRO's salary and fringe benefits,[17] thereby creating a significant financial burden for the school or district. Policies for arming teachers are accompanied by numerous costs, including insurance premiums, background checks, mental health screenings, licensing, training, storage, and even the cost of the weapons themselves.[18] Metal detectors carry a high cost for the initial equipment for a single machine, and schools often need more than one at any given entry point to be able to admit all students into the building in a timely manner. Similarly, while grants may be available to fund the initial cost to purchase security cameras, they do not cover ongoing maintenance costs. Further, both types of equipment require additional financial commitments relative to the personnel necessary to operate them.[19]

A second issue related to these various solutions is their impact on the school community, particularly students, as the presence of security officers and metal detectors has been found to make students more fearful at school[20] and to perceive their environments as unsafe.[21] Moreover, these policies have a disproportionate and negative impact on students of color.[22] One study of New York City schools, for example, found that 48 percent of Black and 38 percent of Hispanic high school students pass through metal detectors in the five boroughs daily; by comparison, just 14 percent of White students do.[23] These devices were found to be more heavily concentrated in schools in the boroughs—Bronx, Brooklyn—with more diverse student populations as well.

Third, there is no evidence to suggest that any one of these solutions is effective, particularly in relation to preventing or responding to school shootings. Both Columbine and Parkland had SROs on campus on the day of the shootings, and in neither school were these individuals successful at ending the attacks. With regard to armed teachers, not only is there a lack of evidence that this policy could achieve its goal of stopping school shootings, there also are concerns that the presence of armed teachers could increase the lethality of an attack because of the lack of training and stress control or the possibility of friendly fire (police mistaking the good

Samaritan for the shooter).[24] Metal detector scans similarly have been found to yield little in the way of results, with just one dangerous item found for every 23,034 scans conducted.[25] By comparison, more weapons have been found in searches conducted without the use of metal detectors.[26] Arguments that entry control measures can prevent mass shootings further fail insofar as the majority of the perpetrators are students and therefore will already be in the building without having to go through added access points, and would not be flagged as someone who did not belong at the school. While each of these measures may provide visible security, their impact on school shootings and on safety more broadly remains largely questionable.

Beyond building-level measures, a booming security consumer product market has emerged that has capitalized on the fear and concern over mass shootings in schools. Among the numerous bulletproof items introduced into the market have been backpacks, white boards, seat cushions, iPad cases, binders, and even clothing. Ballistics shelters for classrooms and window films have been marketed to schools, as have panic buttons and even gunshot detection systems. Despite high costs and no evidence that any of these products achieves its goals of preserving life during a school shooting, sales continue to soar, particularly after a new attack makes headlines.

CREATING COMPREHENSIVE SCHOOL SAFETY PLANS

School safety and preparedness has a much broader context than lockdown drills or any other one specific practice. An Obama-era presidential directive put forward a national preparedness strategy that included five mission areas of emergency preparedness: prevention, protection, mitigation, response, and recovery.[27] *Prevention* starts before an event and entails having the capabilities in place to avoid or stop a threat. *Protection* emphasizes securing against threats (violence, disasters) and may include exterior door locks, firewalls on computers and networks, student supervision, and visitor control systems, some of which also can be considered preventative. *Mitigation* focuses on reducing the impact of threats (e.g., through the use of emergency protocols, such as evacuation, or warning systems to increase preparedness). *Response* includes saving lives, protecting property, and meeting basic needs after an incident. Finally, *recovery* involves assisting schools and communities in rebuilding infrastructure and restoring natural, health, social, and cultural resources and services.[28]

Guidance from the US Department of Education emphasizes the importance of comprehensive planning for schools and districts seeking to develop or update their emergency operations plans.[29] Most prevention, protection, and mitigation activities occur before an emergency occurs, though they have ongoing applicability throughout an incident. Response activities typically occur during an incident, while recovery begins during an emergency event and may continue in the days, weeks, months, and even years after its conclusion.[30] For ease of reference, preparedness activities for schools typically are categorized into what happens before, during, and after an incident.

Long before an emergency incident occurs, it is essential that a collaborative, multidisciplinary safety team engages in careful planning that considers multiple threats and hazards, all settings and times (e.g., events on- and off-campus, such as sporting events, before, during, and after school), and provides for access and functional needs of the entire school community. Schools should use the National Incident Management System's Incident Command System (ICS) to develop a standardized response.[31] The ICS identifies the roles that may be needed to respond to an incident, including the command staff (incident commander, public information officer, liaison officer, and security officer), operations, planning, logistics, and finance and administration. By implementing the ICS, which can be adapted to a wide variety of threats and hazards, schools should be able to engage in a more efficient and effective response; the ICS structure also allows a common language and framework to be used when collaborating with other agencies, which serves to improve coordination of efforts.[32]

Comprehensive prevention and protection efforts to create safe schools should balance physical and psychological safety with efforts to create and maintain a positive school climate.[33] Physical safety planning in schools can be guided by the principles of CPTED described earlier,[34] including natural surveillance (e.g., adult monitoring, security cameras), access control (locked doors, identification and screening of visitors), and territoriality (a clean, welcoming school). Increases in students' perceptions of safety and a reduction in violent behaviors have both been associated with schools' adherence to CPTED principles.[35] In addition, multitiered systems of support can be used to implement evidence-based prevention and intervention approaches that increase in intensity based on student needs; these, as well as school mental health services and threat assessment and management teams (to address suicide and other behavioral concerns), are all part of comprehensive school safety approaches.[36]

Emergency operations plans (EOPs) also are a critical part of comprehensive preparedness efforts. EOPs consist of functional annexes, or critical operations and courses of action, that span prevention, protection, mitigation, and response. These can include response strategies such as lockdown, evacuation, and shelter-in-place protocols, in addition to accounting for all persons, relaying warnings and other pertinent communications, and family reunification plans. Other functional annexes specifically address response and recovery. The continuity of operations annex, for example, helps to ensure that essential functions (e.g., payroll, purchasing, communication, teaching and learning, facilities maintenance, computer and systems support) continue to be performed both during and immediately after a crisis. Similarly, the public health, medical, and mental health annex establishes the specific courses of action that schools should implement to be able to address these issues in emergency situations. Recovery is an essential consideration for schools, and safety teams must plan for the academic, physical, fiscal, psychological, and emotional aspects that may need attention long after the crisis is over.

NO "ONE-SIZE-FITS-ALL" APPROACH

In an ideal world, we would be able to point to one single recommendation (or even a focused group of proposals) that could address the various emergency situations that schools must plan for. The reality is that safety and preparedness efforts must be as layered and complex as the threats themselves.

As this chapter illustrates, many considerations must be taken into account when designing a school's emergency operations plan, and such efforts must take into account a host of factors, including the types of threats the building is susceptible to and the available resources. There are, however, guiding principles that can be used to structure such efforts, as well as best practices related not only to lockdowns but also to other strategies that may be included in school safety plans. In the concluding chapter, we offer several key takeaways, based on the information presented in this book, that can be used to guide schools in their emergency preparedness efforts.

10

THE FUTURE OF LOCKDOWNS AND OTHER EMERGENCY PREPAREDNESS DRILLS

Key Takeaways

- It is important to have an ongoing dialogue about school safety not only among educators but with students as well.
- Continual practice is important for building skill mastery, and assessment is needed to identify areas for improvement.
- Schools should prepare for a range of emergencies, both general (e.g., fires, active attackers) and those more specific to their area (e.g., weather hazards), as well as other crises (suicide, bullying) that may affect the school community.
- Standardizing response protocols can ensure greater predictability during an emergency.

Lockdown drills have been a common feature in the US educational system since the 1999 shooting at Columbine High School, much as reading, writing, and arithmetic are part of the curriculum. In the more than twenty years since the nation watched in horror as two seniors held their school captive, ultimately taking the lives of twelve classmates and a teacher before taking their own, students and educators have prepared in case they too are faced with such an attack, just as they have prepared for other emerging threats. For many, these skills are never called on; for some, the preparedness efforts of their schools have ensured that they have lived to learn or teach another day. Even events like the January 6, 2021, insurrection at the US Capitol highlight the benefits of training in lockdown drills. When the building was stormed by a violent mob, the training of many younger staffers from their time in elementary and secondary schools helped save not only their lives but also the lives many of the nation's congressional representatives.[1]

The continued occurrence of school shootings and other acts of school-based violence ultimately necessitates lockdown drills as one of a number of tools to help minimize the loss of life if the worst day were to happen. They also prepare schools for a host of other internal threats that may be more likely. Although rare, events like the Columbine shooting and the Capitol riot highlight what is perhaps the most important lesson about lockdown drills, and emergency preparedness training more broadly: it is better to have the tools to respond and not need them than to need them and not have them. In this concluding chapter, we offer five key takeaways about how to think and talk about lockdown drills moving forward, as outlined in figure 10.1. We also call on fellow researchers to continue building a foundation of evidence to inform such practices so that schools do them as effectively as possible.

HAVE THE HARD CONVERSATIONS

Talking about school safety, and especially the situations that would trigger a real-world lockdown, is difficult. No one

10.1 Key takeaways related to lockdown drills and school safety. *Note:* Checkmark icon licensed under Creative Commons (Attribution 3.0 Unported).

wants to think about the worst possible scenario happening in their school. Yet the reality is that people *are* thinking about it. Public opinion polls have found that school shootings are a worry for students and their parents alike.[2] It is as well for teachers,[3] though to a lesser extent (probably as a function of educators typically being more likely than their students to perceive their schools as safe).

Numerous factors contribute to the worry over school shootings, including (but certainly not limited to) their high-profile media coverage media and how these tragedies are discussed and analyzed on social media. At the same time, students growing up as members of "Generation Columbine" understand, even if not fully, what has shaped their experiences . . . and they have questions. *What happens if someone forgets to lock the door? What if the shooter pretends to be a police officer? What if they climb through the air vents and get into our room? What if we are outside on the playground,*

in the bathroom, or in the hallway? What if someone gets shot?
These are just a few of the many questions we have encountered from students in our time working with schools on
lockdown drills.

Hearing these questions is hard, but providing the answers
is necessary. There often may be a hesitancy to have these
conversations with students. After all, they are just children,
and they should be allowed to just be kids, right? Yet because
they do not know a world free of these practices, their questions are natural and a function of their experiences, so providing answers—in an age-appropriate manner and with the
guidance of school psychologists and other trauma-informed
experts—can help increase their feelings of safety, perceived
preparedness, and overall well-being. At the same time, their
knowing that their concerns are being listened to and vali-
dated is an important part of the empowerment process.

One of the main ways in which these questions and
concerns can be addressed is through training, as this can
increase buy-in from both students and their teachers. As
we have noted, it is not sufficient just to tell people to perform certain steps of the lockdown process. Providing them
with additional information, namely, why these steps are
performed and their importance in the bigger picture, will
increase the likelihood that people will complete the action
correctly and take the overall practice seriously. Training sessions, particularly when conducted in group settings, remind
everyone of their individual responsibilities during a crisis,
as well as what to expect from others, so that efforts may be
more coordinated. They also allow time for additional questions to be asked and answered.

PRACTICE MAKES PROGRESS

Although in an ideal world, lockdown drills and other emergency preparedness practices would be carried out perfectly 100 percent of the time, in the real world such an expectation is unrealistic. There always will be some margin of error in human activities. Yet, while perfection may be unattainable, improvement is not. Continued practice not only serves to reinforce important points, such as steps to be taken by the individual and the collective in a lockdown drill, it also creates opportunities to identify areas that need improvement. With careful evaluation of the drills, school administrators and safety teams can pinpoint specific areas in need of attention, introduce measures to address these concerns, such as additional training, and reassess to determine whether the strategies implemented fixed the issue or whether further action is needed. It is important to remember that emergency preparedness is a dynamic rather than a static process. All planning and practice should take this into account.

Similarly, it is crucial that schools vary their drills in terms of timing. It is easy to practice a lockdown drill when everyone is tucked neatly into a classroom. It is much more difficult to conduct the same practice during arrival, dismissal, class changes, or the lunch period, which also happen to be times when school shootings are more likely to occur.[4] Although scheduling non-classroom drills may require more from the school and those charged with ensuring the integrity of the drill, it is important to create opportunities to assess the functionality of the response strategy. Moreover, varying the time and location of the drill ensures that participants do not become complacent or expect a drill, which can easily defeat the purpose of the practice and potentially undermine its integrity. As famed circus founder and showman P. T. Barnum has been quoted as saying, "Comfort is the enemy of progress."

Each and every practice is an opportunity for learning. As vital as it is to highlight the opportunities for improvement, it is just as important to call attention to the actions being done correctly. Every member of the school has a vested interest in the drill being done correctly and to the best of everyone's ability. Since an emergency response is not the responsibility of a single individual but of all, it is critical to emphasize the role of collective responsibility in addition to individual accountability to improve coordination and buy-in. Slow progress, even small changes made each time a drill is conducted, is still progress—and it is better than no growth or improvement at all.

PREPARE FOR ALL HAZARDS

School shootings, though tragic, are exceedingly rare. When preparing for emergencies, therefore, schools should plan and practice not only for the very worst day but for all potential threats and hazards they may encounter.[5] While lockdown drills, for example, can be used to prepare for any threat inside the building, including angry parents and dangerous animals in addition to active assailants, they are not necessarily sufficient to address the nuances of other types of emergencies. The actions taken during a lockdown would not be used in instances of a weather-related emergency, such as a tornado or earthquake. Similarly, the actions taken during a lockdown would not be used in the event of a fire, where evacuating the building would be more appropriate.

The all-hazards approach to emergency preparedness planning has been promoted by government entities, including the Centers for Disease Control and Prevention,[6] the Federal Emergency Management Agency,[7] and the Department of Homeland Security,[8] and made applicable to schools through the collaboration of the US Department of Education and the Readiness and Emergency Management for Schools (REMS) Technical Assistance Center.[9] At the core of the approach is the recognition that not only are entities such as schools vulnerable to a number of different types of threats but also that these hazards will vary based on location. Accordingly, identifying and prioritizing response planning for the potential threats more likely to emerge in one's specific situation is imperative. Planning for as many different hazards or threats as possible is important because it is impossible to know in advance exactly what scenarios each school will face. Vulnerability or risk assessments can assist with this process, but strategies for prevention and the potential impacts of any threat also should be considered. Importantly, school administrators and safety teams should plan not only for what to do during the crisis but also what to do prior to the event (prevention) and after it has ended (reunification and recovery).

STANDARDIZATION IS KEY

Unfortunately, at the time of this writing, there is little in the way of national guidance as to what lockdown drills should look like. While best practices and recommendations are available from groups like the National Association of

School Psychologists and the National Association of School Resource Officers,[10] it is unclear how frequently these recommendations are consulted or incorporated into school-level plans. Consequently, there is considerable variability in how response practices are conducted and what protocols are used. This issue arises not only at the national level but also at the state and even district level.

Adopting a national standard or, at the very least, a consistent protocol for a district is critical to the success of emergency preparedness efforts as it helps increase the predictability of responses.[11] In other words, even in situations such as active shooter events that are dynamic in nature, having a standardized plan in place ahead of time can increase the likelihood of a predictable response. This standardized response is helpful both for those experiencing the crisis and for the first responders who will be arriving on scene to provide assistance. When the threat or hazard is neutralized and the event comes to a conclusion, having a standardized, predictable plan can help restore order more quickly and facilitate a smoother recovery process. Moreover, research has suggested that predictability in emergency response planning actually can reduce the risk of harm.[12] When determining how best to standardize the response plans within and between schools, administrators and policymakers should consult both research findings and the best practices promulgated by various bodies to establish guiding principles.

PLAN NOT ONLY FOR THE WORST DAY BUT FOR EVERY DAY

Finally, as schools engage in the planning and preparedness for various threats and hazards, it is important to focus not only on those that make national news headlines and lead to a demand for responses, such as school shootings, but also on the bigger picture of the myriad possible challenges faced by students and their educators. Youth homicides, for example, are less likely to occur at school compared to other locations, with fewer than 2 percent of such incidents taking place in educational institutions each year.[13] Significantly more common issues faced by schools are youth suicide,[14] which is the second leading cause of death among school-aged children after accidents and unintentional injuries,[15] and bullying, an issue that affects at least one out of every five students.[16] Having policies and procedures, such as threat assessment and management teams, can help identify students in crisis and get them the necessary resources to deescalate the situation.[17] Since many school shooters have felt bullied and also have either contemplated or attempted suicide,[18] such protocols also can help identify individuals with a propensity for violence and create opportunities to prevent them from carrying out an attack.

School personnel should always prioritize student wellbeing, along with the welfare of faculty, staff, and administrators, and develop comprehensive approaches to address any such concerns.[19] These strategies can easily complement policies related to active shooter responses or lockdown drills instead of being supplemental to them. In other words, rather than hyperfocusing on the threat least likely to occur, school shootings, grounding related response strategies in a big-picture approach to school safety will help provide the necessary context for students and educators to view their schools as safe places rather than the next target. A contextualized approach also should help promote a culture of preparedness within the schools.

A CALL TO RESEARCHERS

Ensuring that policies and procedures introduced into the school environment are based on evidence and research must be a priority for school administrators, parents, and other vested stakeholders. Lockdown drills are no exception to this principle, particularly in light of their widespread use nationwide. Implementing such practices without incorporating these foundational guidelines can be detrimental to those who take part in them; so too, however, can be abolishing them without in-depth assessment of their impacts. While the work highlighted in this book provides a starting point for building an evidence base, considerable work remains for the research community to do.

There are several avenues of inquiry that can and should be pursued as we move forward in the conversation about lockdown and school safety drills. First, research should be conducted with schools in different types of communities. Most of the research to date has been conducted in a large urban school district. Drills conducted in schools in suburban or rural communities may have a different impact as a result of various factors, such as poverty level or degree of parental involvement.

Second, researchers should consider the additional impacts of these practices on those who participate in them. Broadly, such assessments may consider such outcomes as academic performance, attendance rates, or school discipline concerns. They also may consider the impacts of participating in lockdown drills for groups that are particularly vulnerable in schools, such as students of color or individuals with disabilities, as these practices may exacerbate social, emotional, or behavioral issues. Students with physical disabilities may face difficulties in complying with the steps of the procedure; these limitations should be identified and a tailored response plan developed before a crisis happens.

Finally, there is considerable variability in the protocols being used across the nation that warrants further assessment to understand the impact of these practices. Whether a lockdown drill or one of the various active shooter protocols—A.L.I.C.E., Avoid Deny Defend, Run Hide Fight—is being practiced, the goal is largely the same: to keep students and their educators safe in times of crisis. What remains unknown, however, is how these various protocols may be affecting school communities differently. Such information is necessary to guide discussions about best practices, with an eye toward establishing uniform guidance for our nation's schools to ensure that the drills are being done with care and fidelity.

SOME FINAL THOUGHTS

No one wants to think about their community becoming the next Littleton, Newtown, or Parkland. Yet one of the most dangerous perspectives in the broader conversation about school shootings is the belief (or perhaps the desire to believe) that "it could never happen here." Viewing these tragedies as some other community's problem can create a false sense of safety, which may result in a complacent attitude toward ensuring that emergency preparedness protocols are in place and that everyone who works or studies in the school, as well as first responders in the community, is up to date on them. Though schools and communities need not live in fear of whether "today is the day," they do need to properly plan and prepare for multiple threats and hazards, just as they do for fires, despite the rarity of deaths attributable to school building fires.[20]

Decisions about how best to prepare schools for *any* emergency, including an active attacker, are not made easily or lightly. More important, such decisions are not made in a vacuum. They require careful planning and attention to a number of different considerations, as we have outlined in the previous chapters. We hope this book provides all vested stakeholders—policymakers, school administrators, faculty, staff, parents, and students—with the information needed to be able to have an open and critical dialogue about the status of lockdown drills and emergency preparedness in their schools.

APPENDIX
ANNUAL DRILL REQUIREMENTS BY STATE FOR LOCKDOWNS OR OTHER EMERGENCIES

State	Lockdown or Equivalent Required	Additional Guidance
Alabama AL Code § 16-1-44 (2019) AL Code § 36-19-10 (2019)	Yes	One emergency drill is required per month; includes fire, weather, or code red (threats and/or acts of school violence). At least one code red drill must be conducted within the first six weeks of each semester.
Alaska AK Stat. § 14.03.140 (2019) AK Stat. § 14.33.100 (2019)	Yes (in part)	One evacuation drill is required per month (weather permitting). Lockdown drills are not mandated by law but fall under training requirements for district employees (not for students).
Arizona AZ Rev. Stat. § 15-341(A)(31) (2019) Arizona Department of Education School Emergency Operations Plans (EOP) Minimum Requirements (2019)	Yes	Schools are required to conduct three lockdown drills annually, one of which shall take place while students are outside the classroom. Schools also are required to conduct one shelter-in-place drill annually; monthly fire drills are required, with one conducted during the first week of the school year.
Arkansas AR Code § 6-15-1303 (2019) AR Code § 6-10-121 (2019)	Yes	Active shooter drills are to be conducted annually as part of a school safety assessment in collaboration with local law enforcement and emergency management. At least one lockdown drill must be conducted in conjunction with panic button alert systems training. Tornado safety drills are required a minimum of three times per year, in September, January, and February.

California CA Educ. Code § 32282 (2019) CA Educ. Code § 32001 (2019)	No	California Senate Bill 541 gives the state until November 1, 2021, to research and decide on school drills to be required statewide. Fire drills are required monthly for elementary grades, four times per year for intermediate grades, and at least twice per year at secondary level.
Colorado CO Rev. Stat. § 22-32-109.1 (2019)	Not specifically	"All hazards drills" (of which lockdown is a part) should be conducted, in addition to fire drills, but no additional guidance is given. Fire drills are conducted within ten days of the first day of school, and then monthly thereafter. Two fire drills can be replaced with another drill (e.g., a lockdown drill).
Connecticut CT Gen. Stat. § 10–231 (2019)	Not specifically	A "crisis drill" (not lockdown specifically) is required to be substituted for a fire drill once every three months. The format should be chosen in consultation with law enforcement officials. Fire drills are conducted within thirty days of the first day of school and then monthly thereafter.
Delaware 29 DE Code § 8237 (2019)	Yes	At least two lockdown/intruder drills are required per school year. An additional tabletop exercise is required to be conducted annually.

(continued)

State	Lockdown or Equivalent Required	Additional Guidance
District of Columbia District of Columbia Public Schools School Emergency Response Plan and Management Guide (2010)	Yes	Schools are required to conduct at least two lockdown drills annually. Additional requirements include at least two emergency evacuation and one severe weather drill annually, as well as monthly fire drills, with at least two conducted during the first two weeks of the school year.
Florida FL Stat. § 1006.07 (2019)	Yes	Drills for active shooter and hostage situations shall be conducted at least as often as other emergency drills (no specific number is required).
Georgia GA Code § 20-2-1185 (2019)	Not specifically	School safety drills should be conducted, but the form and frequency will be determined by guidance from the Georgia Emergency Management and Homeland Security Agency.
Hawaii Required by Hawaii State Department of Education	Yes	All schools are required to conduct drills for lockdowns, shelter-in-place, evacuation (including fire); earthquakes, and tsunamis; the frequency is not specified.
Idaho Id. Admin. Code r. 08.02.03.160 (2014) Fire Code 2015 of Idaho	No	Fire/evacuation drills are required to be conducted within ten days of the first day of school and then monthly thereafter.

State / Citation	Active shooter drill required	Requirements
Illinois 105 ILCS 128/15 (2019) 105 ILCS 128/20 (2019)	Yes	Schools must conduct at least one "law enforcement drill" within the first 90 days of the school year to address an active threat or active shooter in the school. Schools also must conduct a minimum of three drills for school evacuation/fires, one for bus evacuation, one for severe weather, and one for shelter-in-place.
Indiana IN Code § 20-34-3-20 (2019)	Yes	Schools must conduct at least one "manmade occurrence disaster drill" per semester. They also must conduct at least one tornado preparedness drill in the same period. These drills may be conducted in place of monthly required fire drills but may not be conducted as consecutive replacements.
Iowa IA Code § 280.30 (2019) IA Code § 100.31 (2019)	Not specifically	Schools are required to conduct a minimum of one drill based on emergency operations plan. This drill may include an active shooter drill and a natural disasters drill. A minimum of four fire and four tornado drills also are required annually.
Kansas KS Stat. § 31–133 (2019)	Not specifically	Schools are required to conduct three crisis drills per year; these drills may cover active shooters but also earthquakes, hazardous spills, or medical emergencies. Schools also must conduct at least two tornado drills (one each in September and March) and four fire drills annually.

(continued)

State	Lockdown or Equivalent Required	Additional Guidance
Kentucky KY Rev. Stat. § 158.164 (2019) KY Rev. Stat. § 158.163 (2019)	Yes	Lockdown drills are required to be conducted at least two times per year; one must be held within the first thirty days of the school year and the other in January. Schools also are required to conduct practices for drop procedures (used for earthquakes and tornadoes) and safe area evacuations at the same frequency and timing as lockdown drills.
Louisiana LA Rev. Stat. § 17:416.16 (2019)	Not specifically	Schools are required to conduct at least one safety drill annually within the first thirty days of the school year. The crisis management and response plan being practiced in the safety drill should include guidance for active shooters, but the drill is not required to cover practice specifically related to these events.
Maine 05–071 CMR chap. 125, § 5.17 (2019)	Yes	Schools are required to conduct both lockdown and emergency evacuation drills, but the law does not identify how many of each. Two drills must be held during the first two weeks of school for all K–12 levels. The number of additional drills varies between four and eight, depending on the grade level.
Maryland Md. Code Regs. 13A.02.02.04 (2020)	Yes	Lockdown drills, as well as practices for evacuation, reverse evacuation, shelter-in-place, severe weather, and drop, cover, and hold, shall be conducted annually in addition to fire drills; the specific frequency is not stated.

State	Active shooter/lockdown drills required	Requirements
Massachusetts Massachusetts Comprehensive Fire Safety Code—School Fire Drills, 527 CMR 1.00 MA Gen. L. chap. 90 § 7b (2019)	No	The state has no requirement for active shooter or lockdown drills to be conducted in schools. Schools are required to have four fire drills conducted by the local fire department and two on-bus evacuation drills per year.
Michigan MI Comp. L. § 29.19 (2019)	Not specifically	A minimum of three drills must be conducted that involve the building occupants to secure inside (this may be the equivalent of a lockdown, lockout, or shelter-in-place drill); at least one must be conducted by December 1 and one after January 1. A minimum of five fire drills are required annually (three in the fall and two in the remainder of the school year), as are two tornado safety drills.
Minnesota MN Stat. § 121A.035 (2019)	Yes	Schools must conduct at least five lockdowns annually as part of their crisis management plan. In addition, schools must conduct at least five fire drills and one tornado drill.
Mississippi MS Code § 37-11-5 (2019)	Yes	Two lockdown/active shooter drills are required annually. At least one of the drills must be conducted within the first sixty days of the start of a new school year. Fire drills are required to be conducted monthly and tornado drills at least two times per year.

(continued)

State	Lockdown or Equivalent Required	Additional Guidance
Missouri MO Rev. Stat. § 170.315 (2019)	Yes (in part)	All school personnel are required to take part in a simulated active shooter/intruder response drill conducted by law enforcement personnel; students are not required to participate, and the frequency of the drill is not stipulated.
Montana MT Code § 20-1-401 (2019) MT Code § 20-1-402 (2019)	Not specifically	Schools are required to conduct at least eight "disaster drills" annually at different times. The type of hazards that will be the focus of the drills is left up to individual school districts to decide, based on independent risk assessments.
Nebraska NE Code § 79–609 (2019) NE Code § 79–2,144 (2019) NE Fire Safety Code 15.7.1	No	Schools are recommended, but not required, to conduct drills for lockdowns and lockouts. Schools are required to conduct monthly fire drills with one additional evacuation drill taking place in the first thirty days of the school year, as well as two tornado/shelter drills (one during the first two weeks of school and the other during March) and two bus evacuation drills.
Nevada NV Rev. Stat. § 392.450 (2019)	Yes	Monthly drills are required for either lockdown, fire, or other emergency procedures. At least half of the drills conducted must be lockdowns, and no more than three can be focused on responses to chemical explosions, other similar emergencies, or natural disasters.

New Hampshire NH Rev. Stat. § 189:64 (2019)	Yes	At least four of the required number of fire evacuation drills must be emergency, all-hazard response drills; at least one of these must be focused on armed assailant response.
New Jersey NJ Rev. Stat. § 18A:41–1 (2019)	Not specifically	Schools are required to conduct at least one fire and one "school security drill" monthly. School security drills may focus on active shooters, as well as bomb threats, lockdowns, and nonfire evacuations. At least one of the school security drills must be assessed by a law enforcement officer.
New Mexico NM Stat. § 22-13-14 (2019)	Yes	During the first four weeks of the school year, schools are required to conduct one shelter-in-place drill (for an active shooter response), one evacuation drill, and two fire drills. Four additional emergency drills must be conducted during the remainder of the school year, of which two must be fire drills.
New York NY Educ. L. § 807 (2019)	Yes	Four lockdown drills are required annually. An additional eight evacuation drills must be conducted, with eight total drills (lockdowns and evacuations combined) taking place between September 1 and December 31.
North Carolina NC Gen. Stat. § 115C-105.49 (2019) NC Gen. Stat. § 115C-288 (2019)	Yes	At least one lockdown drill is required annually. Monthly fire drills also are required to be conducted, with the first conducted within the first week of school opening.

(continued)

State	Lockdown or Equivalent Required	Additional Guidance
North Dakota NDCC § 15.1-06-12 (2019)	Yes	Schools are required to conduct lockdown and tornado drills each year; the frequency of each is not specified. A minimum of four fire/emergency evacuation drills is required annually, with the first conducted within ten days of classes beginning.
Ohio Ohio Rev. Code § 3737.73 (2019)	Yes	School safety drills must be conducted at least three times per year with at least one such drill to include a scenario (e.g., active shooter) in which students must be secured within the school building. Schools also must conduct at least six "drills or rapid dismissals" for evacuations in response to a sudden emergency each year.
Oklahoma 70 OK Stat § 5–148 (2019) 70 OK Stat. § 5–149 (2019)	Yes	Schools are required to conduct a minimum of four "security drills" (e.g., lockdowns, intruder drills) per school year; the latter must be conducted within the first fifteen days of each semester. A minimum of six additional drills are required annually: two must be fire drills conducted within the first fifteen days of each semester; two tornado drills, with one in September and one in March; and the remaining two drills at the discretion of the principal or superintendent based on risks to the specific school or district.

Oregon OR Rev. Stat. § 336.071 (2019)	Yes	At least two drills for "safety threats" (lockdowns) are required annually. Safety threat plans also must include guidance for lockouts, shelter-in-place events, and evacuation. Schools also must conduct monthly fire drills, with the first completed within ten days of the start of the school year. At least two earthquake drills are required per year. Schools in a tsunami hazard zone must conduct three earthquake and tsunami drills per school year.
Pennsylvania 24 P.S. § 15–1517	Not specifically	One "school security drill" is required to be conducted annually in place of a fire drill within ninety days of the beginning of the school year; following the ninety-day period, one additional security drill may be conducted in lieu of one fire drill. Fire drills must be conducted no less than once per month.
Rhode Island RI Gen. L. § 16-21-4 (2019)	Yes	Two lockdown drills are required annually, one in September and one in January. An additional two evacuation drills shall be conducted annually, as well as monthly emergency egress (fire) drills.
South Carolina SC Code § 59-63-910 (2019)	Yes	At least two active shooter/intruder drills must be conducted annually, with at least one in each semester. At least two fire drills and two severe weather/earthquake drills also must be conducted annually (one per semester).

(continued)

State	Lockdown or Equivalent Required	Additional Guidance
South Dakota SD Codified L. § 13-25-10 (2019)	No	No state requirement for lockdown drills exists; some districts do have specific requirements for lockdowns (e.g., Sioux Falls requires at least one per year, along with at least one tornado drill per semester). Schools are required to conduct at least two fire/evacuation drills per semester.
Tennessee TN Code § 49-6-807 (2019) TN Code § 68-102-137 (2019)	Yes	At least one armed intruder drill must be conducted annually and in coordination with the appropriate local law enforcement agency. Schools also must conduct at least one fire drill per month plus one additional fire drill within the first thirty days of the school year. Three additional safety drills (e.g., inclement weather, earthquake, intruder) must be conducted during the school year.
Texas TX Educ. Code § 37.114 (2019) 19 Tex. Admin. Code § 103.1209 (2020)	Yes	Schools are required to conduct two lockdown drills per year, one per semester. Schools also must conduct the following drills each school year: one secure/lockout drill, one evacuation drill, one shelter-in-place drill for hazmat, one shelter-in-place drill for severe weather, and four fire drills (two per semester).

Utah Utah Admin. Code R277–400-6 (2020) UT Code § 15A-5–202.5 (2019)	Yes	All schools are required to conduct at least one lockdown drill during the school year. Elementary schools are required to conduct emergency drills at least once per month, while secondary schools are required to conduct four drills per year. The first drill of the school year must be a fire drill and must be conducted within the first ten days of the school year. An additional fire drill must be conducted within ten days of students returning from winter break.
Vermont 16 V.S.A. § 1481 (2019) VT Fire & Building Safety Code	Yes	Schools are required to conduct at least one fire or emergency preparedness drill per month. Per 2016 guidance from the Vermont Fire & Building Safety Code, schools were required to conduct six evacuation drills and five lockdown drills annually.
Virginia VA Code § 22.1–137.2 (2019) VA Code § 22.1–137.1 (2019) VA Code § 22.1–137 (2019)	Yes	Schools are required to conduct at least two lockdown drills within the first twenty days of each school session, with at least one additional lockdown drill conducted after the first sixty days of the session. Schools also are required to conduct at least two fire drills within the first twenty days of each school session, with at least two additional fire drill during the remainder of the school session; at least one tornado drill must be conducted annually.

(continued)

State	Lockdown or Equivalent Required	Additional Guidance
Washington WA Rev. Code § 28A.320.125 (2019)	Yes	Schools are required to conduct at least one safety-related drill per month, including the summer months, to practice lockdowns, shelter in place (for limiting exposure to hazardous materials), and evacuation (for fires and tsunamis). There is no specific requirement for the number of each type of drill to be conducted.
West Virginia WV Emergency Management Crisis Response Plan Guidance Office of the State Fire Marshall (firemarshal.wv.gov)	Yes	Schools are required to participate in at least one lockdown drill per year. If more are conducted, it is recommended that one take place while class is in session and the other when it is not. Schools also are recommended to conduct at least one shelter-in-place drill per school year. Schools are required to conduct two fire drills within the first thirty days of the school year, with one additional drill monthly thereafter.
Wisconsin WI Stat. § 118.07 (2019)	Yes	Schools are required to conduct a minimum of two school safety/intruder drills annually; a safety drill may also be substituted for any other required drill. Schools also must conduct two evacuation drills (for tornadoes or other hazards) annually; fire drills are required monthly.
Wyoming WY Stat. § 35-9-505 (2019)	Not specifically	"Safety drills" (not lockdowns specifically) may be conducted in lieu of fire drills provided that the latter are conducted no less than four times per academic year and that any changes are approved by and coordinated with the local fire department. Fire drills are required to be conducted at least once every month.

Note: Information is current as of February 27, 2021.

NOTES

CHAPTER 1

1. Arika Herron, "'It Hurt So Bad': Indiana Teachers Shot with Plastic Pellets during Active Shooter Training," *IndyStar*, March 22, 2019, https://www.indystar.com/story/news/politics/2019/03/21/active-shooter-training-for-schools-teachers-shot-with-plastic-pellets/3231103002; Karen Zraick, "Indiana Teachers Were Shot with Pellets during Active-Shooter Drill, Union Says," *New York Times*, March 22, 2019, https://www.nytimes.com/2019/03/22/us/indiana-teachers-shot.html.

2. Ed Richter, "Shotgun Blanks to Be Shot Inside School Today as Part of Drill," *Dayton Daily News*, October 1, 2019, https://www.daytondailynews.com/news/shotgun-blanks-shot-inside-school-today-part-drill/YzcCV3bXeJA3tM35oZyIHL.

3. George Pierpoint, "US School Shootings: Have Drills Gone Too Far?," *BBC News*, March 31, 2019, https://www.bbc.com/news/uk-47711020; Scott Poland, "Keep Schools Safe: Planning Plays a Key Role in Preventing School Violence," *American School Board Journal* 203, no. 4 (2016): 24–25, https://psychology.nova.edu/news-events/SchoolBoardJournalKeepingSchoolsSafe.pdf.

4. Evie Blad and Madeline Will, "Some Left 'Traumatized' by Training Tactics," *Education Week*, March 24, 2019, https://www.edweek.org/ew/articles/2019/03/24/i-felt-more-traumatized-than-trained-active-shooter.html.

5. Lauren Musu, Anlan Zhang, Ke Wang, Jizhi Zhang, and Barbara A. Oudekerk, "Indicators of School Crime Safety: 2018" (US Department

of Education and US Department of Justice, 2019), https://nces.ed
.gov/pubs2019/2019047.pdf.

6. Everytown for Gun Safety, "The Impact of School Safety Drills for
Active Shootings" (2020), https://everytownresearch.org/school-safety
-drills.

7. Lauren Rygg, "School Shooting Simulations: At What Point Does
Preparation Become More Harmful Than Helpful?," *Children's Legal
Rights Journal*, 35, no. 3 (2015): 215–228.

8. Centers for Disease Control and Prevention, "Data and Statistics
on Children's Mental Health," 2020, https://www.cdc.gov/childrens
mentalhealth/data.html.

9. Reem M. Ghandour, Laura J. Sherman, Catherine J. Vladutiu, Mir
M. Ali, Sean E. Lynch, Rebecca H. Bitsko, and Stephen J. Blumberg,
"Prevalence and Treatment of Depression, Anxiety, and Conduct
Problems in US Children," *Journal of Pediatrics* 206 (2019): 256–267,
https://doi.org/10.1016/j.jpeds.2018.09.021.

10. Steven Rich and John Woodrow Cox, "'What If Someone Was
Shooting?,'" *Washington Post*, December 26, 2018, https://www
.washingtonpost.com/graphics/2018/local/school-lockdowns-in
-america.

11. Steven Rich and John Woodrow Cox, "Scarred by School Shootings," *Washington Post*, March 25, 2018, https://www.washingtonpost
.com/graphics/2018/local/us-school-shootings-history.

12. Jaclyn Schildkraut, Margaret K. Formica, and Jim Malatras. "Can
Mass Shootings Be Stopped? To Address the Problem, We Must Better
Understand the Phenomenon," policy brief (Rockefeller Institute of
Government, 2018), http://rockinst.org/wp-content/uploads/2018/05
/5-22-18-Mass-Shootings-Brief.pdf.

13. Kristin M. Holland, Jeffrey E. Hall, Jing Wang, Elizabeth M. Gaylor,
Linda L. Johnson, Daniel Shelby, Thomas R. Simon, and School-
Associated Violent Deaths Study Group, "Characteristics of School-
Associated Youth Homicides—United States, 1994–2018," *Morbidity and
Mortality Weekly Report* 68, no. 3 (2019): 53–60, https://doi.org/10.15585
/mmwr.mm6803a1.

14. Marjory Stoneman Douglas High School Public Safety Commission, "Initial Report Submitted to the Governor, Speaker of the House

of Representatives, and Senate President" (2019), https://www.fdle
.state.fl.us/MSDHS/CommissionReport.pdf.

15. Paula M. Di Nota and Juha-Matti Huhta, "Complex Motor Learning and Police Training: Applied, Cognitive, and Clinical Perspectives,"
Frontiers in Psychology 10 (2019): 1–20, https://doi.org/10.3389/fpsyg
.2019.01797; Richard Shusterman, "Muscle Memory and the Somaesthetic Pathologies of Everyday Life," *Human Movement* 12, no. 1 (2011):
4–15, https://doi.org/10.2478/v10038-011-0001-2.

CHAPTER 2

1. Lauren Musu, Anlan Zhang, Ke Wang, Jizhi Zhang, and Barbara A.
Oudekerk, "Indicators of School Crime Safety: 2018" (US Department
of Education and US Department of Justice, 2019), https://nces.ed
.gov/pubs2019/2019047.pdf.

2. Steven Rich and John Woodrow Cox, "'What If Someone Was
Shooting?,'" *Washington Post*, December 26, 2018, https://www.wash
ingtonpost.com/graphics/2018/local/school-lockdowns-in-america.

3. David McCullough, *Truman* (Simon & Schuster, 1992).

4. Richard Rhodes, *Arsenals of Folly: The Making of the Nuclear Arms
Race* (Vintage Books, 2007).

5. JoAnne Brown, "'A Is for Atom, B Is for Bomb': Civil Defense in
American Public Education, 1948–1963," *Journal of American History*
75, no. 1 (1988): 68–90, https://doi.org/10.2307/1889655.

6. The video (9 minutes and 15 seconds) can be viewed at https://
archive.org/details/DuckandC1951.

7. Jessica Carella, "When the Angels Came Calling," *NFPA Journal*
(2008), https://www.nfpa.org/News-and-Research/Publications-and
-media/NFPA-Journal/2008/July-August-2008/Features/When-the
-Angels-Came-Calling.

8. Sarah Crosswy, "The Collinwood School Disaster Influenced Fire
Safety Protocols" (National Museum of American History, 2016),
https://americanhistory.si.edu/blog/collinwood-disaster-fire-safety;
Carter Jones, "The Cleveland School Fire of 1923" (South Carolina
State Firefighter's Association, 2015), https://scfirefighters.org/the-cleve
land-school-fire-of-1923.

9. A. E. Winship, "Fire Drills in Chicago," *Journal of Education* 102, no. 16 (1925): 431–433, https://www.jstor.org/stable/42831988.

10. Melissa Allen Heath, Katherine Ryan, Brenda Dean, and Rebecka Bingham, "History of School Safety and Psychological First Aid for Children," *Brief Treatment and Crisis Intervention* 7, no. 3 (2007): 206–223, http://dx.doi.org/10.1093/brief-treatment/mhm011.

11. US Department of Education, "Safety: 5 Ways to Learn about Fire Safety" (2015), https://www2.ed.gov/free/features/fire-safety.html.

12. National Fire Protection Association, "US School Fires, Grades K–12, with 10 or More Deaths" (n.d.), https://www.nfpa.org/News -and-Research/Data-research-and-tools/Building-and-Life-Safety /Structure-fires-in-schools/US-school-fires-with-ten-or-more-deaths.

13. Richard Campbell, "Structure Fires in Schools" (National Fire Protection Association, 2020), https://www.nfpa.org//-/media/Files/News -and-Research/Fire-statistics-and-reports/Building-and-life-safety /osSchools.pdf.

14. Ke Wang, Yongqiu Chen, Jizhi Zhang, and Barbara A. Oudekerk, "Indicators of School Crime and Safety: 2019" (National Center for Education Statistics, 2020), https://nces.ed.gov/pubs2020/2020063.pdf.

15. "I Love U Guys" Foundation, "The Standard Response Protocol K–12: Operational Guidance for Implementing the Standard Response Protocol in a K–12 Environment" (2020), https://iloveuguys.org/The -Standard-Response-Protocol.html.

16. Kathleen B. Asparanti, Taylor K. Pelchar, Daniel F. McCleary, Sherry K. Bain, and Lisa N. Foster, "Development and Reliability of the Comprehensive Crisis Plan Checklist," *Psychology in the Schools* 48, no. 2 (2011): 146–155, https://doi.org/10.1002/pits.20533; Bob Hull, "Changing Realities in School Safety and Preparedness," *Journal of Business Continuity & Emergency Planning* 5, no. 1 (2011): 440–451.

17. US Department of Education, "Natural Disaster Resources" (n.d.), https://www.ed.gov/disasterrelief.

18. National Severe Storms Laboratory, "Learning Resources: for Students" (n.d.), https://www.nssl.noaa.gov/education/students; National Weather Service, "Severe Weather Preparation Guidance for Schools" (n.d.), https://www.weather.gov/grb/schools; Federal Emergency Management Agency, "Protecting School Children from Tornadoes: State

of Kansas School Shelter Initiative" (2002), https://www.fema.gov /sites/default/files/2020-08/protecting_school_children_tornadoes _ks_ssi.pdf.

19. Jaclyn Schildkraut and Glenn W. Muschert, *Columbine, 20 Years Later and Beyond: Lessons from Tragedy* (Praeger, 2019).

20. Columbine Review Commission, "The Report of Governor Bill Owens' Columbine Review Commission," (State of Colorado, 2001), 116, http://hermes.cde.state.co.us/drupal/islandora/object/co:2067/data stream/OBJ/view.

21. National Center for Education Statistics, *Report on Indicators of School Crime and Safety*, https://nces.ed.gov/programs/crimeindicators.

22. US Government Accountability Office, "Most School Districts Have Developed Emergency Management Plans, but Would Benefit from Additional Federal Guidance" (2007), https://www.gao.gov /assets/270/261878.pdf.

23. Navigate 360, "About ALICE: Active Shooter Training & Preparedness Solutions with ALICE" (2021), https://www.alicetraining.com /about-us.

24. Advanced Law Enforcement Rapid Response Training Center, "Avoid Deny Defend" (n.d.), https://www.avoiddenydefend.org.

25. "I Love U Guys" Foundation, "About" (n.d.), https://iloveuguys .org/About.html.

26. US Department of Homeland Security, *Active Shooter: How to Respond* (2008), https://www.dhs.gov/xlibrary/assets/active_shooter_ booklet.pdf.

27. US Department of Education, Office of Elementary and Secondary Education, Office of Safe and Healthy Students, *Guide for Developing High-quality School Emergency Operations Plans* (2013), https:// mk0edsource0y23p672y.kinstacdn.com/wp-content/uploads/old /REMS_K-12_Guide_508.pdf.

28. J. Pete Blair, Terry Nichols, David Burns, and John R. Curnutt, *Active Shooter: Events and Responses* (CRC Press, 2013).

29. Sandy Hook Advisory Commission, "Final Report of the Sandy Hook Advisory Commission" (Hartford, CT: SHAC, 2015), https://portal .ct.gov/-/media/Malloy-Archive/Sandy-Hook-Advisory-Commission /SHAC_Final_Report_3-6-2015.pdf.

30. Chuck Haga, "Woman Lives with Horrors of 2005 Red Lake Shootings, Brought Back by New Tragedy," *Grand Forks Herald*, December 17, 2012, https://www.grandforksherald.com/news/2185456-woman-lives-horrors-2005-red-lake-shootings-brought-back-new-tragedy; "10 Years after Red Lake Shootings, Memories Still Haunt," *Twin Cities Pioneer Press*, March 17, 2015, https://www.twincities.com/2015/03/17/10-years-after-red-lake-shootings-memories-still-haunt.

31. Park County Office of Emergency Management. "Platte Canyon High School Shooting: After Action Report" (Park County, CO, 2006).

32. Terry Spencer, "Investigators: School Design Contributed to Parkland Massacre," *Florida Today*, April 24, 2018, https://www.floridatoday.com/story/news/2018/04/24/investigators-school-design-contributed-parkland-massacre/546961002; Kyle Swenson, and Samantha Schmidt, "'I'm Not Really Shocked': Florida High School Prepared for the Worst. Then It Happened," *Washington Post*, February 15, 2018, https://www.washingtonpost.com/news/morning-mix/wp/2018/02/15/im-not-really-shocked-florida-high-school-prepared-for-the-worst-then-it-happened.

33. School Safety Infrastructure Council, "Report of the School Safety Infrastructure Council: Revised and Updated to June 27, 2014 (Danbury, CT: SSIC, 2014), https://business.ct.gov/-/media/DAS/Communications/SSIC-Report-Nov-19-2015.pdf; National School Shield Task Force, "The Report of the National School Shield Task Force" (National Rifle Association, 2013), https://www.nraschoolshield.org/media/1844/summary-report-of-the-national-school-shield-task-force.pdf. See also M. Hunter Martaindale, William L. Sandel, and J. Pete Blair, "Active-Shooter Events in the Workplace: Findings and Policy Implications," *Journal of Business Continuity & Emergency Planning* 11, no. 1 (2017): 6–20.

34. John Preston, *Disaster Education: "Race," Equity, and Pedagogy* (Sense Publishers, 2012); Victoria A. Johnson, Kevin R. Ronan, David M. Johnston, and Robin Peace, "Evaluations of Disaster Education Programs for Children: A Methodological Review," *International Journal of Disaster Risk Reduction* 9 (2014): 107–123, http://dx.doi.org/10.1016/j.ijdrr.2014.04.001.

35. United Nations Specialized Conferences, "Hyogo Framework for Action 2005–2015: Building the Resilience of Nations and Communities to Disasters" (2005), 9, https://www.refworld.org/docid/42b98a704.html.

36. Farah Mulyasari, Yukiko Takeuchi, and Rajib Shaw, "Implementation tools for Disaster Education," in *Disaster Education,* ed. Rajib Shaw, Kolchi Shiwaku, and Yukiko Takeuchi (Emerald Group Publishing, 2011), 137–151, https://doi.org/10.1108/S2040-7262(2011)0000007013.

37. Paula M. Di Nota, and Juha-Matti Huhta, "Complex Motor Learning and Police Training: Applied, Cognitive, and Clinical Perspectives," *Frontiers in Psychology* 10 (2019): 1–20, https://doi.org/10.3389/fpsyg.2019.01797; Richard Shusterman, "Muscle Memory and the Somaesthetic Pathologies of Everyday Life," *Human Movement* 12, no. 1 (2011): 4–15, https://doi.org/10.2478/v10038-011-0001-2.

38. Jaclyn Schildkraut and Amanda B. Nickerson, "Ready to Respond: Effects of Lockdown Drills and Training on School Emergency Preparedness," *Victims & Offenders* 15, no. 5 (2020): 619–638, https://doi.org/10.1080/15564886.2020.1749199.

39. John D. Vitek and Susan M. Berta, "Improving Perception of and Response to Natural Hazards: The Need for Local Education," *Journal of Geography* 81, no. 6 (1982): 225–228, https://doi.org/10.1080/00221348208980740.

40. Qiangyu Deng, Yipeng Lv, Fangjie Zhao, Wenya Yu, Junqiang Dong, and Lulu Zhang, "Factors Associated with Injuries among Tornado Victims in Yancheng and Chifeng, China," *BMC Public Health* 19 (2019): 1–9, https://doi.org/10.1186/s12889-019-7887-6.

CHAPTER 3

1. US Department of Homeland Security, Federal Emergency Management Agency, "Homeland Security Exercise and Evaluation Program (HSEEP)" (2020), https://training.fema.gov/programs/hseep.

2. US Department of Education, Office of Elementary and Secondary Education, Office of Safe and Healthy Students, "Guide for Developing High-Quality School Emergency Operations Plans" (2013), https://mk0edsource0y23p672y.kinstacdn.com/wp-content/uploads/old/REMS_K-12_Guide_508.pdf.

3. US Department of Education, Office of Elementary and Secondary Education, Office of Safe and Healthy Students, "Guide for Developing High-Quality School Emergency Operations Plans."

4. "I Love U Guys" Foundation, "The Standard Response Protocol K–12" (2021), https://iloveuguys.org/The-Standard-Response-Protocol.html.

5. "I Love U Guys" Foundation, "The Standard Response Protocol K–12," 6.

6. Cheryl Lero Jonson, Melissa M. Moon, and Joseph A. Hendry, "One Size Does Not Fit All: Traditional Lockdown versus Multioption Responses to School Shootings," *Journal of School Violence* 19, no. 2 (2020): 154–166, https://doi.org/10.1080/15388220.2018.1553719.

7. US Department of Justice, Federal Bureau of Investigation, and the Advanced Law Enforcement Rapid Response Training Center at Texas State University, "Active Shooter Incidents in the United States in 2018" (2019), 2, https://www.fbi.gov/file-repository/active-shooter -incidents-in-the-us-2018-041019.pdf.

8. National Association of School Psychologists, National Association of School Resource Officers, and Safe and Sound Schools, *Best Practice Considerations for Armed Assailant Drills in Schools* (2021), https://www .nasponline.org/Documents/Research%20and%20Policy/Advocacy%20 Resources/Armed-Assailant-Guide-FINAL.pdf.

9. US Department of Homeland Security, *Active Shooter: How to Respond* (2008), https://www.dhs.gov/xlibrary/assets/active_shooter_ booklet.pdf.

10. US Department of Homeland Security, Federal Emergency Management Agency, "Be Prepared for an Active Shooter" (2018), https:// www.fema.gov/media-library-data/1523561958719-f1eff6bc841d56b 7873e018f73a4e024/ActiveShooter_508.pdf.

11. Navigate 360, "About ALICE: Active Shooter Training & Preparedness Solutions with ALICE" (2021), https://www.alicetraining.com /about-us; Advanced Law Enforcement Rapid Response Training Center, "Avoid Deny Defend" (Texas State University, n.d.), https://www.avoid denydefend.org.

12. US Department of Homeland Security, Federal Emergency Management Agency, "FEMA—Emergency Management Institute (EMI) Course IS-362.A: Multi-Hazard Emergency Planning for Schools" (2020), https://training.fema.gov/is/courseoverview.aspx?code=IS-362 .a; National Association of School Psychologists, "Conducting Crisis Exercises and Drills: Guidelines for Schools" (2013), https://www .nasponline.org/resources-and-publications/resources-and-podcasts /school-climate-safety-and-crisis/systems-level-prevention/conducting

-crisis-exercises-and-drills; US Department of Education, Office of Elementary and Secondary Education, Office of Safe and Supportive Schools, "The Role of Districts in Developing High-Quality School Emergency Operations Plans" (2019), https://www.ed.gov/school-safety/?src=feature.

13. US Department of Education, Office of Elementary and Secondary Education, Office of Safe and Healthy Students, "Guide for Developing High-Quality School Emergency Operations Plans"; Stephen E. Brock, Amanda B. Nickerson, Melissa A. Reeves, Christina N. Conolly, Shane R. Jimerson, Rosario C. Pesce, and Brian R. Lazzaro, *School Crisis Prevention and Intervention: The PREPaRE Model*, 2nd ed. (Bethesda, MD: National Association of School Psychologists, 2016); "I Love U Guys" Foundation, "The Standard Response Protocol K–12"; Brock et al., *School Crisis Prevention and Intervention*; Dusty Columbia Embury, Laura S. Clarke, and Kim Weber, "Keeping Our Students Safe during Crisis," *Physical Disabilities: Education and Related Services* 38, no. 1 (2019): 1–9, doi: 10.14434/pders.v38i1.27970.

14. US Department of Homeland Security, Federal Emergency Management Agency, "Homeland Security Exercise and Evaluation Program (HSEEP)."

15. National Association of School Psychologists, National Association of School Resource Officers, and Safe and Sound Schools, *Best Practice Considerations for Armed Assailant Drills in Schools*.

16. National Association of School Psychologists, "Best Practice Considerations for Schools in Active Shooter and Other Armed Assailant Drills"; David J. Schonfeld, Marlene Melzer-Lange, Andrew N. Hashikawa, Peter A. Gorski, and American Academy of Pediatrics Council on Children and Disasters, Council on Injury, Violence, and Poison Prevention, Council on School Health, "Participation of Children and Adolescents in Live Crisis Drills and Exercises," *Pediatrics* 146, no. 3 (2020), e2020015503, https://doi.org/10.1542/peds.2020-015503.

17. "I Love U Guys" Foundation, "The Standard Response Protocol K–12"; Schonfeld et al., "Participation of Children and Adolescents in Live Crisis Drills and Exercises"; Partner Alliance for Safer Schools, "Safety and Security Guidelines for K–12 Schools" (2020), https://passk12.org/guidelines-resources/pass-school-security-guidelines.

CHAPTER 4

1. US Department of Education, Office of Elementary and Secondary Education, Office of Safe and Healthy Students, "Guide for Developing High-Quality School Emergency Operations Plans" (2013), https://mk0edsource0y23p672y.kinstacdn.com/wp-content/uploads/old/REMS_K-12_Guide_508.pdf.

2. Safe Havens International, "Know the Drill—Safe and Effective School Emergency Operations Exercises" (n.d.), https://safehavensinternational.org/services/presentations/school-crisis-response-plans/know-the-drill-safe-and-effective-school-emergency-operations-exercises.

3. John-Michael Keyes, "The Standard Reunification Method," presentation at the Winter Briefings, "I Love U Guys" Foundation, Wheat Ridge, Colo., February 2020.

4. National Association of School Psychologists, "Conducting Crisis Exercises and Drills: Guidelines for Schools" (2013), https://www.nasponline.org/resources-and-publications/resources-and-podcasts/school-climate-safety-and-crisis/systems-level-prevention/conducting-crisis-exercises-and-drills.

5. Kenneth S. Trump, "School Safety in a Post-Sandy Hook World" (Education Commission of the States, 2014), ERIC No. ED561912, https://eric.ed.gov/?id=ED561912.

6. US Department of Homeland Security, Federal Emergency Management Agency, *Homeland Security Exercise and Evaluation Program (HSEEP)* (2020), https://training.fema.gov/programs/hseep.

7. US Department of Education, Office of Elementary and Secondary Education, Office of Safe and Healthy Students, "Guide for Developing High-Quality School Emergency Operations Plans"; US Department of Education, Office of Elementary and Secondary Education, Office of Safe and Supportive Schools, "The Role of Districts in Developing High-Quality School Emergency Operations Plans" (2019), https://www.ed.gov/school-safety/?src=featurel.

8. Readiness and Emergency Management for Schools Technical Assistance Center, "Mitigation for Schools and School Districts" (2017), https://rems.ed.gov/Docs/Mitigation_Fact_Sheet_508C.pdf.

9. US Department of Education, "Final Report of the U.S. Federal Commission on School Safety" (2018), https://www2.ed.gov/documents/schoolsafety/school-safety-report.pdf.

10. Victoria A. Johnson, Kevin R. Ronan, David M. Johnston, and Robin Peace, "Evaluations of Disaster Education Programs for Children: A Methodological Review," *International Journal of Disaster Risk Reduction* 9 (2014): 107–123, http://dx.doi.org/10.1016/j.ijdrr.2014.04.001.

11. Yechiel Soffer, Avishay Goldberg, Galit Avisar-Shohat, Robert Cohen, and Yaron Bar-Dayan, "The Effect of Different Educational Interventions on Schoolchildren's Knowledge of Earthquake Protective Behaviour in Israel," *Disasters* 34, no. 1 (2010): 205–213, doi: 10.1111/j.1467-7717.2009.01125.x.

12. Amanda B. Nickerson and Jaclyn Schildkraut, "State Anxiety Prior to and after Participating in Lockdown Drills among Students in a Rural High School," *School Psychology Review* (2021), https://doi.org /10.1080/2372966X.2021.1875790; Jaclyn Schildkraut and Amanda B. Nickerson, "Ready to Respond: Effects of Lockdown Drills and Training on School Emergency Preparedness," *Victims and Offenders* 15, no. 5 (2020): 619–638, https://doi.org/10.1080/15564886.2020 .1749199; Jaclyn Schildkraut, Amanda B. Nickerson, and Thomas Ristoff, "Locks, Lights, Out of Sight: Assessing Students' Perceptions of Emergency Preparedness across Multiple Lockdown Drills," *Journal of School Violence* 19, no. 1 (2020), 93–106, https://doi.org/10.1080 /15388220.2019.1703720.

13. Donna L. Floyd, Steven Prentice-Dunn, and Ronald W. Rogers, "A Meta-Analysis of Research on Protection Motivation Theory," *Journal of Applied Social Psychology* 30, no. 2 (2000): 407–429, https://doi.org /10.1111/j.1559-1816.2000.tb02323.x.

14. Schildkraut and Nickerson, "Ready to Respond"; Schildkraut, Nickerson, and Ristoff, "Locks, Lights, Out of Sight."

15. US Department of Homeland Security, *Active Shooter: How to Respond* (2008), https://www.dhs.gov/xlibrary/assets/active_shooter_ booklet.pdf.

16. Sandy Hook Advisory Commission, "Final Report of the Sandy Hook Advisory Commission" (Hartford, CT: SHAC, 2015), https://portal .ct.gov/-/media/Malloy-Archive/Sandy-Hook-Advisory-Commission /SHAC_Final_Report_3-6-2015.pdf.

17. Melissa Martin, "No More Sitting Ducks," *The Post*, September 29, 2013, https://www.thepostnewspapers.com/brunswick/local_news/no -more-sitting-ducks/article_2d9c4e7f-4297-5562-a47e-a7e924131f2f .html.

18. Cheryl Lero Jonson, Melissa M. Moon, and Joseph A. Hendry, "One Size Does Not Fit All: Traditional Lockdown versus Multi-option Responses to School Shootings," *Journal of School Violence* 19, no. 2 (2020): 154–166, https://doi.org/10.1080/15388220.2018.1553719.

19. US Department of Homeland Security, *Active Shooter: How to Respond.*

20. US Department of Education, Office of Elementary and Secondary Education, Office of Safe and Healthy Students, "Guide for Developing High-Quality School Emergency Operations Plans."

21. Jonson, Moon and Hendry, "One Size Does Not Fit All."

22. Michael Dorn, "Dangers of Active Shooter Training Programs" (2018), https://higherlogicdownload.s3.amazonaws.com/NBOA/Uploaded Images/c781eb1f-9fca-4408-b2f8-9bceec57f0af/NetAssets/2018/10/Dorn-SS-SO18.pdf.

23. Cheryl Lero Jonson, Melissa M. Moon, and Brooke Miller Gialopsos, "Are Students Scared or Prepared? Psychological Impacts of a Multi-option Active Assailant Protocol Compared to Other Crisis/emergency Preparedness Practices," *Victims & Offenders* 15, no. 5 (2020): 639–662, https://doi.org/10.1080/15564886.2020.1753871.

24. National Association of School Psychologists, "NASP and NASRO Urge Accuracy with Regard to Lockdown versus Other types of Armed Assailant Drills" (February 16, 2020), https://www.nasponline.org/about-school-psychology/media-room/press-releases/nasp-and-nasro-urge-accuracy-with-regard-to-lockdown-versus-other-types-of-armed-assailant-drills.

25. Everytown for Gun Safety Support Fund, American Federation of Teachers, and National Education Association, "Keeping Our Schools Safe: A Plan to Stop Mass Shootings and End All Gun Violence in American Schools" (2020), https://everytownresearch.org/school-safety-plan.

26. Mahita Gajanan, "Alaska's Students Will Be Taught How to Evade a School Shooter," *Time*, August 28, 2016, https://time.com/4469968/alaskas-alice-student-school-shooter-evade; Sylvia Varnham O'Regan, "The Company behind America's Scariest School Shooter Drills," *The Trace*, December 13, 2019, https://www.thetrace.org/2019/12/alice-active-shooter-training-school-safety.

27. "I Love U Guys" Foundation, "The Standard Response Protocol K–12" (2021), https://iloveuguys.org/programs/standard-response -protocol-for-k-12.

28. Everytown for Gun Safety, "The Impact of School Safety Drills for Active Shootings" (2020), https://everytownresearch.org/school -safety-drills; David J. Schonfeld, Marlene Melzer-Lange, Andrew N. Hashikawa, Peter A. Gorski, and American Academy of Pediatrics Council on Children and Disasters, Council on Injury, Violence, and Poison Prevention, Council on School Health, "Participation of Children and Adolescents in Live Crisis Drills and Exercises," *Pediatrics* 146, no. 3 (2020), e2020015503, https://doi.org/10.1542/peds.2020-015503.

29. Erika Christakis, "Active-Shooter Drills Are Tragically Misguided," *Atlantic*, March 13, 2019. www.theatlantic.com/magazine/archive /2019/03/active-shooter-drills-erikachristakis/580426.

30. George Pierpoint, "US School Shootings: Have Drills Gone Too Far?," *BBC News*, March 31, 2019, https://www.bbc.com/news/uk-47711020.

31. Dewey Cornell, "Our Schools Are Safe: Challenging the Misperception That Schools Are Dangerous Places," *American Journal of Orthopsychiatry* 85, no. 3 (2015): 217–220, https://doi.org/10.1037 /ort0000064; Dorn, Dangers of Active Shooter Training Programs."

32. Everytown for Gun Safety Support Fund, American Federation of Teachers, and National Education Association, "Keeping Our Schools Safe"; Andrew Yang, "End Active Shooter Drills—Yang2020—Andrew Yang for President" (n.d.), https://www.yang2020.com/policies/end -active-shooter-drills.

33. National Association of School Psychologists, National Association of School Resource Officers, and Safe and Sound Schools, *Best Practice Considerations for Armed Assailant Drills in Schools* (2021), https://www .nasponline.org/Documents/Research%20and%20Policy/Advocacy%20 Resources/Armed-Assailant-Guide-FINAL.pdf; Schonfeld et al., "Participation of Children and Adolescents in Live Crisis Drills and Exercises."

34. Schonfeld et al., "Participation of Children and Adolescents in Live Crisis Drills and Exercises."

CHAPTER 5

1. Richard Luscombe, "Generation Columbine: How Mass Shootings Changed America's Schools," *Guardian*, April 19, 2019. https://www

.theguardian.com/us-news/2019/apr/19/columbine-parkland-how
-mass-shootings-changed-us-schools; Greg Toppo, "'Generation Columbine' Has Never Known a World without School Shootings," *USA
Today*, February 22, 2018, https://www.usatoday.com/story/news/2018
/02/22/generation-columbine-has-never-known-world-without-school
-shootings/361656002.

2. Jaclyn Schildkraut, "Can Mass Shootings Be Stopped? To Address
the Problem, We Must Better Understand the Phenomenon," policy
brief (Rockefeller Institute of Government, 2021), https://rockinst.org
/issue-area/2021-can-mass-shootings-be-stopped.

3. Everytown for Gun Safety, American Federation of Teachers, and
National Education Association, "Keeping Our Schools Safe: A Plan
for Preventing Mass Shootings and Ending All Gun Violence in American Schools" (2020), https://everytownresearch.org/report/a-plan-for
-preventing-mass-shootings-and-ending-all-gun-violence-in-american
-schools.

4. Evie Blad and Madeline Will, "'I Felt More Traumatized Than
Trained': Active-Shooter Drills Take Toll on Teachers," *Education Week*,
March 24, 2019, https://www.edweek.org/ew/articles/2019/03/24/i-felt
-more-traumatized-thantrained-active-shooter.html; Rhitu Chatterjee,
"A Look at the Impact of Active Shooter Drills," National Public Radio,
June 5, 2019, https://www.npr.org/2019/06/05/730057542/a-look-at
-the-impact-of-active-shooter-drills; Steven Rich and John Woodrow
Cox, "'What If Someone Was Shooting?,'" *Washington Post*, December 26, 2018, https://www.washingtonpost.com/graphics/2018/local
/school-lockdowns-in-america; Lauren Rygg, "School Shooting Simulations: At What Point Does Preparation Become More Harmful Than
Helpful?," *Children's Legal Rights Journal*, 35, no. 3 (2015): 215–228,
http://lawecommons.luc.edu/clrj/vol35/iss3/3.

5. Joseph A. Simonetti, "Active Shooter Safety Drills and Students—
Should We Take a Step Back?," *JAMA Pediatrics* 174, no. 11 (2020):
1021–1022, https://doi.org/10.1001/jamapediatrics.2020.2592.

6. Cheryl Lero Jonson, Melissa M. Moon, and Brooke Miller Gialopsos, "Are Students Scared or Prepared? Psychological Impacts of
a Multi-Option Active Assailant Protocol Compared to Other Crisis/
emergency Preparedness Practices," *Victims & Offenders* 15, no. 5
(2020): 639–662, https://doi.org/10.1080/15564886.2020.1753871.

7. Guiherme V. Polanczyk, Giovanni A. Salum, Luisa S. Sugaya, Arthur Caye, and Luis A. Rohde, "Annual Research Review: A Meta-analysis of the Worldwide Prevalence of Mental Disorders in Children and Adolescents," *Journal of Child Psychology and Psychiatry* 56, no. 3 (2015): 345–365, https://doi.org/10.1111/jcpp.12381.

8. Reem M. Ghandour, Laura J. Sherman, Catherine J. Vladutiu, Mir M. Ali, Sean E. Lynch, Rebecca H. Bitsko, and Stephen J. Blumberg, "Prevalence and Treatment of Depression, Anxiety, and Conduct Problems in US Children," *Journal of Pediatrics* 206 (2019): 256–267, https://doi.org/10.1016/j.jpeds.2018.09.021.

9. Natalie Slopen, Garrett M. Fitzmaurice, David R. Williams, and Stephen E. Gilman, "Common Patterns of Violence Experiences and Depression and Anxiety among Adolescents," *Social Psychiatry and Psychiatric Epidemiology* 47, no. 10 (2012): 1591–1605, https://doi.org/10.1007/s00127-011-0466-5.

10. Wanda P. Fremont, "Childhood Reactions to Terrorism-induced Trauma: A Review of the Past 10 Years," *Journal of the American Academy of Child and Adolescent Psychiatry* 43, no. 4 (2004): 381–392, https://doi.org/10.1097/00004583-200404000-00004; Kevin R. Ronan, David M. Johnston, Michele Daly, and Raewyn Fairley, "School Children's Risk Perceptions and Preparedness: A Hazards Education Survey," *Australasian Journal of Disaster and Trauma Studies* (2001), no. 1, http://trauma.massey.ac.nz/issues/2001-1/ronan.htm.

11. Mary E. Woesner, "The Return of Duck and Cover and the Imminence of Death—What It Means for Physicians," *JAMA Pediatrics* 172, no. 6 (2018): 511–512, https://doi.org/10.1001/jamapediatrics.2018.0120.

12. David J. Schonfeld, Eric Rossen, and Diann Woodard, "Deception in Schools—When Crisis Preparedness Efforts Go Too Far," *JAMA Pediatrics* 171, no. 11 (2017): 1033–1034, https://doi.org/10.1001/jamapediatrics.2017.2565.

13. Evie Blad, "Do Schools' 'Active-Shooter' Drills Prepare or Frighten?," *Education Digest* 83, no. 6 (2018): 4–8; David J. Schonfeld, Marlene Melzer-Lange, Andrew N. Hashikawa, Peter A. Gorski, and American Academy of Pediatrics Council on Children and Disasters, Council on Injury, Violence, and Poison Prevention, Council on School Health, "Participation of Children and Adolescents in Live Crisis Drills and

Exercises," *Pediatrics* 146, no. 3 (2020), e2020015503, https://doi.org/10
.1542/peds.2020-015503.

14. Elizabeth J. Zhe and Amanda B. Nickerson, "Effects of an Intruder
Crisis Drill on Children's Knowledge, Anxiety, and Perceptions of
School Safety," *School Psychology Review* 36, no. 3 (2007): 501–508,
https://doi.org/10.1080/02796015.2007.12087936.

15. Charles D. Spielberger and Richard Gorsuch, *Manual for the State-
trait Anxiety Inventory (Form Y)* (Consulting Psychologists Press, 1983).

16. Amanda B. Nickerson and Jaclyn Schildkraut, "State Anxiety Prior
to and after Participating in Lockdown Drills among Students in a
Rural High School," *School Psychology Review* (2021), https://doi.org
/10.1080/2372966X.2021.1875790.

17. Patrick Sylvers, Scott O. Lilienfeld, and Jamie L. LaPrairie, "Differences between Trait Fear and Trait Anxiety: Implications for Psy-
chopathology," *Clinical Psychology Review* 31, no. 1 (2011): 122–137,
https://doi.org/10.1016/j.cpr.2010.08.004.

18. Kenneth F. Ferraro, *Fear of Crime: Interpreting Victimization Risk*
(State University of New York Press, 1995).

19. Lynn A. Addington, "Students' Fear after Columbine: Findings
from a Randomized Experiment," *Journal of Quantitative Criminology* 19,
no. 4 (2003): 367–387, https://doi.org/10.1023/B:JOQC.0000005440
.11892.27; Nancy D. Brener, T.homas R. Simon, Mark Anderson, Lisa
C. Barrios, and Meg L. Small, "Effect of the Incident at Columbine on
Students' Violence- and Suicide-Related Behaviors," *American Journal
of Preventive Medicine* 22, no. 3 (2002): 146–150; R. K. Kaminski, B. A.
Koons-Witt, N. S. Thompson, and D. Weiss, "The Impacts of the Virginia Tech and Northern Illinois University Shootings on Fear of Crime
on Campus," *Journal of Criminal Justice* 38, no. 1 (2010): 88–98, https://
doi.org/10.1016/j.jcrimjus.2009.11.011.

20. Ronet Bachman, Antonia Randolph, and Bethany L. Brown, "Predicting Perceptions of Fear at School and Going to and from School
for African American and White Students: The Effect of School Security Measures," *Youth & Society* 43, no. 2 (2011): 705–726, https://doi
.org/10.1177/0044118X10366674.

21. Michael G. Huskey and Nadine M. Connell, "Preparation or
Provocation? Student Perceptions of Active Shooter Drills," *Criminal*

Justice Policy Review, 32, no. 1 (2021): 3–26, https://doi.org/10.1177/0887403419900316.

22. Jillian Peterson, Ellen Sackrison, and Angela Polland, "Training Students to Respond to Shootings on Campus: Is It Worth It?," *Journal of Threat Assessment and Management* 2, no. 2 (2015): 127–138, http://dx.doi.org/10.1037/tam0000042.

23. Jonson, Moon and Gialopsos, "Are Students Scared or Prepared?"

24. Suzanne E. Perumean-Chaney and Lindsay M. Sutton, "Students and Perceived School Safety: School Security Measures," *American Journal of Criminal Justice* 38, no. 4 (2013): 570–588. https://doi.org/10.1007/s12103-012-9182-2.

25. N'dea Moore-Petinak, Marika Waselewski, Blaire Alma Patterson, and Tammy Chang, "Active Shooter Drills in the United States: A National Study of Youth Experiences and Perceptions," *Journal of Adolescent Health* 67, no. 4 (2020): 509–513, https://doi.org/10.1016/j.jadohealth.2020.06.015.

26. Jonson, Moon and Gialopsos, "Are Students Scared or Prepared?"

27. Zhe and Nickerson, "Effects of an Intruder Crisis Drill on Children's Knowledge, Anxiety, and Perceptions of School Safety."

28. Jaclyn Schildkraut, Amanda B. Nickerson, and Thomas Ristoff, "Locks, Lights, Out of Sight: Assessing Students' Perceptions of Emergency Preparedness across Multiple Lockdown Drills," *Journal of School Violence* 19, no. 1 (2020), 93–106. https://doi.org/10.1080/15388220.2019.1703720.

29. John H. Laub and Janet L. Lauritsen, "The Interdependence of School Violence with Neighborhood and Family Conditions," in *Violence in American Schools: A New Perspective*, ed. Delbert S. Elliott, Beatrix A. Hamburg, and Kirk R. Williams (Cambridge University Press, 1998), 127–155.

30. Michael Gubiotti, "Opposing Viewpoints: Preparing Students, Teachers, and the Community for School Shootings: Saving Lives with Active Shooter Simulations," *Children's Legal Rights Journal* 35, no. 3 (2015): 254–255. https://lawecommons.luc.edu/clrj/vol35/iss3/6.

31. Moore-Petinak et al., "Active Shooter Drills in the United States."

32. Peterson, Sackrison, and Polland, "Training Students to Respond to Shootings on Campus."

33. Jonson, Moon and Gilopsos, "Are Students Scared or Prepared?"

34. Jaclyn Schildkraut and Amanda B. Nickerson, "Ready to Respond: Effects of Lockdown Drills and Training on School Emergency Preparedness," *Victims and Offenders* 15, no. 5 (2020): 619–638. https://doi.org/10.1080/15564886.2020.1749199; Schildkraut, Nickerson, and Ristoff, "Locks, Lights, Out of Sight."

35. Russell T. Jones and Jeff Randall, "Rehearsal-plus: Coping with Fire Emergencies and Reducing Fire-related Fears," *Fire Technology* 30, no. 4 (1994): 432–444, https://doi.org/10.1007/BF01039942.

36. Keith J. Zullig, "Active Shooter Drills: A Closer Look at Next Steps," *Journal of Adolescent Health* 67, no. 4 (2020): 465–466, https://doi.org/10.1016/j.jadohealth.2020.07.028.

37. Donna L. Floyd, Steven Prentice-Dunn, and Ronald W. Rogers, "A Meta-Analysis of Research on Protection Motivation Theory," *Journal of Applied Social Psychology* 30, no. 2 (2000): 407–429, https://doi.org/10.1111/j.1559-1816.2000.tb02323.x.

38. Schonfeld, Rossen, and Woodard, "Deception in Schools."

CHAPTER 6

1. Kris Bosworth, Lysbeth Ford, and Diley Hernandez, "School Climate Factors Contributing to Student and Faculty Perceptions of Safety in Select Arizona Schools," *Journal of School Health* 81, no. 4 (2011): 191–202, https://doi.org/10.1111/j.1746-1561.2010.00579.x.

2. Brandon J. Wood and Eric Hampton, "The Influence of School Resource Officer Presence on Teacher Perceptions of School Safety and Security," *School Psychology Review* (2021), https://doi.org/10.1080/2372966X.2020.1844547; Sarah J. Rippetoe, "Teachers' and Students' Perceptions about the Roles of School Resource Officers in Maintaining School Safety," PhD diss., East Tennessee State University, 2009.

3. Sondra G. Estep, "Crisis Planning: Building Enduring School-community Relationships," *International Journal for Professional Educators* 79, no. 3 (2013): 13–20, 13.

4. Jaclyn Schildkraut, Amanda B. Nickerson, and Kirsten R. Klingaman, "Reading, Writing, Responding: Educators' Perceptions of Safety, Preparedness, and Lockdown Drills," *Educational Policy* (2021), https://doi.org/10.1177/08959048211015617.

5. Carole Frances Rider, "Teachers' Perceptions of Their Ability to Respond to Active Shooter Incidents," PhD diss., University of Southern Mississippi, 2015.

6. International Association of Chiefs of Police, *Guide for Preventing and Responding to School Violence*, 2nd ed. (Alexandria, VA: International Association of Chiefs of Police, 2009), 4, https://bja.ojp.gov/sites/g/files /xyckuh186/files/Publications/IACP_School_Violence.pdf.

7. Travis D. Embry-Martin, "Perceptions in Preparing for and Responding to an Active Shooter Incident: A Qualitative Study of K–12 Teachers' Self-Efficacy," PhD diss., Northcentral University, 2017; V. Worthington, "Active Shooter Protocols and Training: Effects on University Faculty and Staff," undergraduate thesis, Winthrop University, 2020.

8. James Graham, Steve Shirm, Rebecca Liggin, Mary E. Aitken, and Rhonda Dick, "Mass-Casualty Events at Schools: A National Preparedness Survey," *Pediatrics* 117, no. 1 (2006): 8–15, https://doi.org/10 .1542/peds.2005-0927; M. Kano and L. B. Bourque, "Experiences with Preparedness for Emergencies and Disasters among Public Schools in California," *NASSP Bulletin* 91, no. 3 (2007): 201–218, https://doi.org /10.1177/0192636507305102.

9. Kevin R. Clark, Suzieann M. Bass, and Sonja K. Boiteaux, "Survey of Educators' Preparedness to Respond to Active Shooter Incidents," *Radiologic Technology* 90, no. 6 (2019): 541–551. https://pubmed.ncbi .nlm.nih.gov/31270255.

10. Min Liu, Isaac Blankson, and Laurel S. Brooks, "From Virginia Tech to Seattle Pacific U: An Exploratory Study Regarding Risk and Crisis Preparedness among University Employees," *Atlantic Journal of Communication* 23, no. 4 (2015): 211–224, https://doi.org/10.1080 /15456870.2015.1069683.

11. Jane C. Perkins, "Preparing Teachers for School Tragedy: Reading, Writing, and Lockdown," *Journal of Higher Education Theory and Practice* 18, no. 1 (2018): 70–81, http://m.www.na-businesspress.com /JHETP/JHETP18-1/PerkinsJC_18_1.pdf.

12. Bethney Bergh, "A Qualitative Study of School Lockdown Procedures and Teachers' Ability to Conduct and Implement them at the Classroom Level," PhD diss., Western Michigan University, 2009.

13. Jaclyn Schildkraut and Amanda B. Nickerson, "Ready to Respond: Effects of Lockdown Drills and Training on School Emergency

Preparedness," *Victims and Offenders* 15, no. 5 (2020): 619–638, https://doi.org/10.1080/15564886.2020.1749199; Schildkraut, Nickerson, and Klingaman, "Reading, Writing, Responding."

14. "I Love U Guys" Foundation, "The Standard Response Protocol (SRP) for K–12 Schools" (n.d.), https://iloveuguys.org/The-Standard-Response-Protocol.html.

15. Rider, "Teachers' Perceptions of Their Ability to Respond to Active Shooter Incidents,"

16. New York Education Law § 807, Fire and Emergency Drills (rev. 2019).

17. Monte Gagliardi, Marianne Neighbors, Caile Spears, Scott Byrd, and Jamin Snarr, "Emergencies in the School Setting: Are Public School Teachers Adequately Trained to Respond?," *Prehospital and Disaster Medicine* 9, no. 4 (1994): 222–225, https://doi.org/10.1017/S1049023X00041431.

18. Megumi Kano, Marizen Ramirez, William J. Ybarra, Gus Frias, and Linda B. Bourque, "Are Schools Prepared for Emergencies? A Baseline Assessment of Emergency Preparedness in Three Los Angeles County School Districts," *Education and Urban Society* 39, no. 3 (2007): 399–422, https://doi.org/10.1177/0013124506298130.

19. Department of Homeland Security, "Stop the Bleed" (July 14, 2020), https://www.dhs.gov/stopthebleed.

20. Allison R. Jones, Michelle R. Brown, Amanda Esslinger, Virginia S. Strickland, and Jeffrey D. Kerby, "Evaluation of 'Stop the Bleed' Training among K–12 Faculty and Staff in Alabama," *Public Health Nursing* 36, no. 5 (2019): 660–666, https://doi.org/10.1111/phn.12638; Roy Lei, Michael D. Swartz, John A. Harvin, Bryan A. Cotton, John B. Holcomb, Charles E. Wade, and Sasha D. Adams, "Stop the Bleed Training Empowers Learners to Act to Prevent Unnecessary Hemorrhagic Death," *American Journal of Surgery* 217, no. 2 (2019): 368–372, https://doi.org/10.1016/j.amjsurg.2018.09.025.

21. Perkins, "Preparing Teachers for School Tragedy."

22. Ke Wang, Yongqiu Chen, Jizhi Zhang, and Barbara A. Oudekerk, "Indicators of School Crime and Safety: 2019" (National Center for Education Statistics, 2020), https://nces.ed.gov/pubs2020/2020063.pdf.

23. Elisha Fieldstadt, "Teacher Sues Oregon School District for Traumatic Active-shooter Drill," *NBC News*, April 21, 2015, https://www

.nbcnews.com/news/us-news/teacher-sues-oregon-elementary-school
-traumatic-active-shooter-drill-n345631.

24. Karen Zraick, "Indiana Teachers Were Shot with Pellets during
Active-Shooter Drill, Union Says," *New York Times*, March 22, 2019,
https://www.nytimes.com/2019/03/22/us/ndiana-teachers-shot
.html.

25. Melissa L. Ricketts, "K–12 Teachers' Perceptions of School Policy
and Fear of School Violence," *Journal of School Violence* 6, no. 3 (2007):
45–67, https://doi.org/10.1300/J202v06n03_04.

26. National Association of School Psychologists, National Association
of School Resource Officers, and Safe and Sound Schools, *Best Practice
Considerations for Armed Assailant Drills in Schools* (2021), https://
www.nasponline.org/Documents/Research%20and%20Policy/Advo
cacy%20Resources/Armed-Assailant-Guide-FINAL.pdf.

27. Benjamin I. Bass, Konstantin P. Cigularov, Peter Y. Chen, Kimberly L. Henry, Rocco G. Tomazic, and Yiqiong Li, "The Effects of
Student Violence against School Employees on Employee Burnout
and Work Engagement: The Roles of Perceived School Unsafety and
Transformational Leadership," *International Journal of Stress Management* 23, no. 3 (2016): 318–336, https://psycnet.apa.org/doi/10.1037
/str0000011.

28. Sonali Rajan and Charles C. Branas, "Arming Schoolteachers: What
Do We Know? Where Do We Go from Here?," *American Journal of Public
Health* 108, no. 7 (2018): 860–862, https://ajph.aphapublications.org
/doi/10.2105/AJPH.2018.304464.

CHAPTER 7

1. Richard Shusterman, "Muscle Memory and the Somaesthetic Pathologies of Everyday Life," *Human Movement* 12, no. 1 (2011): 4–15, https://
doi.org/10.2478/v10038-011-0001-2.

2. Kristine M. Gebbie, Joan Valas, Jacqueline A. Merrill, and Stephen
S. Morse, "Role of Exercises and Drills in the Evaluation of Public
Health in Emergency Response," *Prehospital and Disaster Medicine* 21,
no. 3 (2006): 173–182, https://doi.org/10.1017/S1049023X00003642.

3. Marizen Ramirez, Katrina Kubicek, Corinne Peek-Asa, and Marleen
Wong, "Accountability and Assessment of Emergency Drill Performance

in Schools," *Family and Community Health* 32, no. 2 (2009), 105–114, https://doi.org/10.1097/FCH.0b013e3181994662.

4. David Johnston, Ruth Tarrant, Karlene Tipler, Maureen Coomer, Sandy Pedersen, and Ruth Garside, "Preparing Schools for Future Earthquakes in New Zealand: Lessons from an Evaluation of a Wellington School Exercise," *Australian Journal of Emergency Management* 26, no. 1 (2011): 24–30, https://ajem.infoservices.com.au/items/AJEM -26-01-06.

5. Kevin R. Ronan and David M. Johnston, *Promoting Community Resilience in Disasters: The Role for Schools, Youth and Families* (Springer, 2005); Kevin R. Ronan, Kylie Crellin, David M. Johnston, Kirsten Finnis, Douglas Paton, and Julia Becker, "Promoting Child and Family Resilience to Disasters: Effects, Interventions, and Prevention Effectiveness," *Children and Youth Environments* 18, no. 1 (2008): 332–353, https://www.jstor.org/stable/10.7721/chilyoutenvi.18.1.0332.

6. Travis D. Embry-Martin, "Perceptions in Preparing for and Responding to an Active Shooter Incident: A Qualitative Study of K–12 Teachers' Self-Efficacy," PhD diss., Northcentral University, 2017.

7. Karlene S. Tipler, Ruth A. Tarrant, David M. Johnston, and Keith F. Tuffin, "New Zealand ShakeOut Exercise: Lessons Learned by Schools," *Disaster Prevention and Management* 25, no. 4 (2016): 550–563, https:// doi.org/10.1108/DPM-01-2016-0018.

8. Karlene Tipler, Ruth Tarrant, David Johnston, and Keith Tuffin, "Are You Ready? Emergency Preparedness in New Zealand Schools," *International Journal of Disaster Risk Reduction* 25 (2017): 324–333, http://dx.doi.org/10.1016/j.ijdrr.2017.09.035.

9. Mahmood Hossieni and Yasamin O. Izadkhah, "Earthquake Disaster Risk Management Planning in Schools," *Disaster Prevention and Management* 15, no. 4 (2006): 649–661, https://doi.org/10.1108 /09653560610686595; Victoria A. Johnson, Kevin R. Ronan, David M. Johnston, and Robin Peace, "Evaluations of Disaster Education Programs for Children: A Methodological Review," *International Journal of Disaster Risk Reduction* 9 (2014): 107–123, http://dx.doi.org/10.1016/j .ijdrr.2014.04.001.

10. Steve Gwynne, Martyn Amos, Max Kinateder, Noureddine Bénichou, Karen Boyce, C. Natalie van der Wal, and Enrico Ronchi, "The

Future of Evacuation Drills: Assessing and Enhancing Evacuee Performance," *Safety Science* 129 (2020), https://doi.org/10.1016/j.ssci.2020.104767.

11. Elizabeth J. Zhe and Amanda B. Nickerson, "Effects of an Intruder Crisis Drill on Children's Knowledge, Anxiety, and Perceptions of School Safety," *School Psychology Review* 36, no. 3 (2007): 501–508, https://doi.org/10.1080/02796015.2007.12087936.

12. Misty Jo Dickson and Kristina K. Vargo, "Training Kindergarten Students Lockdown Drill Procedures Using Behavioral Skills Training," *Journal of Applied Behavioral Analysis* 50, no. 2 (2017): 407–412, https://doi.org/10.1002/jaba.369.

13. Jaclyn Schildkraut and Amanda B. Nickerson, "Ready to Respond: Effects of Lockdown Drills and Training on School Emergency Preparedness," *Victims and Offenders* 15, no. 5 (2020): 619–638, https://doi.org/10.1080/15564886.2020.1749199.

14. Victoria A. Johnson, David M. Johnston, Kevin R. Ronan, and Robin Peace, "Evaluating Children's Learning of Adaptive Response Capacities from ShakeOut, an Earthquake and Tsunami Drill in Two Washington State School Districts," *Journal of Homeland Security & Emergency Management* 11, no. 3 (2014): 347–373, https://doi.org/10.1515/jhsem-2014-0012.

15. Yechiel Soffer, Avishay Goldberg, Galit Avisar-Shohat, Robert Cohen, and Yaron Bar-Dayan, "The Effect of Different Educational Interventions on Schoolchildren's Knowledge of Earthquake Protective Behaviour in Israel," *Disasters* 34, no. 1 (2010): 205–213, doi: 10.1111/j.1467-7717.2009.01125.x.

16. Da-Hye Yeon, Ji-Bum Chung, and Dong-Hyeon Im, "The Effects of Earthquake Experience on Disaster Education for Children and Teens," *International Journal of Environmental Research and Public Health* 17, no. 15 (2020), https://doi.org/10.3390/ijerph17155347.

17. Kevin R. Ronan, Kylie Crellin, and David Johnston, "Correlates of Hazards Education for Youth: A Replication Study," *Natural Hazards* 53, no. 3 (2010): 503–526, https://doi.org/10.1007/s11069-009-9444-6.

18. Cheryl Lero Jonson, Melissa M. Moon, and Brooke Miller Gialopsos, "Are Students Scared or Prepared? Psychological Impacts of

a Multi-option Active Assailant Protocol Compared to Other Crisis/ Emergency Preparedness Practices," *Victims & Offenders* 15, no. 5 (2020): 639–662, https://doi.org/10.1080/15564886.2020.1753871; Readiness and Emergency Management for Schools Technical Assistance Center, "Integrating Drills and Exercises into overall School Emergency Management Planning," 2019, https://rems.ed.gov/docs/ExercisesWebinar_ Presentation_508C.pdf; Kevin. R. Ronan and David M. Johnston, "Hazards Education for Youth: A Quasi-Experimental Investigation," *Risk Analysis* 23, no. 5(2003): 1009–1020, https://doi.org/10.1111/1539 -6924.00377.

19. Amanda B. Nickerson, Michelle L. Serwacki, Stephen E. Brock, Todd A. Savage, Scott A. Woitaszewski, and Melissa A. Louvar Reeves, "Program Evaluation of the PREPaRE School Crisis Prevention and Intervention Training Curriculum," *Psychology in the Schools* 51, no. 5 (2014): 466–479, https://doi.org/10.1002/pits.21757.

20. Megumi Kano, Marizen Ramirez, William J. Ybarra, and Linda B. Bourque, "Are Schools Prepared for Emergencies? A Baseline Assessment of Emergency Preparedness at School Sites in Three Los Angeles County School Districts," *Education and Urban Society* 39, no. 3 (2007): 399–422, https://doi.org/10.1177%2F0013124506298130.

21. Eric Frau, Vittorio Midoro, and Gian M. Pedemonte, "Do Hypermedia Systems Really Enhance Learning? A Case Study in Earthquake Education," *Educational and Training Technology International* 29, no. 1 (1992): 42–51, https://doi.org/10.1080/0954730920290106.

22. Barbara A. Morrongiello, David C. Schwebel, Melissa Bell, Julia Stewart, and Aaron L. Davis, "An Evaluation of The Great Escape: Can an Interactive Computer Game Improve Young Children's Fire Safety Knowledge and Behaviors?," *Health Psychology* 31, no. 4 (2012): 496– 502, https://doi.org/10.1037/a0027779; Meng-Han Tsai, Ming-Chang Wen, Yu-Lien Chang, and Shih-Chung Kang, "Game-Based Education for Disaster Prevention," *AI & Society* 30, no. 4 (2015): 463–475, https://doi.org/10.1007/s00146-014-0562-7.

23. Hamed Seddighi, Sepideh Yousefzadeh, Mónica López López, and Homeira Sajjadi, "Preparing Children for Climate-Related Disasters," *BMJ Paediatrics Open* 4, no. 1 (2020), https://dx.doi.org/10.1136%2Fbm jpo-2020-000833.

CHAPTER 8

1. Everytown for Gun Safety, *The Impact of School Safety Drills for Active Shootings* (2020), https://everytownresearch.org/school-safety-drills; "I Love U Guys" Foundation, "The Standard Response Protocol K–12" (2021), https://iloveuguys.org/The-Standard-Response-Protocol.html; National Association of School Psychologists, National Association of School Resource Officers, and Safe and Sound Schools, *Best Practice Considerations for Armed Assailant Drills in Schools* (2021), https://www.nasponline.org/Documents/Research%20and%20Policy/Advocacy%20Resources/Armed-Assailant-Guide-FINAL.pdf; US Department of Education, Office of Elementary and Secondary Education, Office of Safe and Healthy Students, "Guide for Developing High-quality School Emergency Operations Plans" (2013), https://www.dhs.gov/sites/default/files/publications/REMS%20K-12%20Guide%20508_0.pdf.

2. David J. Schonfeld, Marlene Melzer-Lange, Andrew N. Hashikawa, Peter A. Gorski, and American Academy of Pediatrics Council on Children and Disasters, Council on Injury, Violence, and Poison Prevention, Council on School Health, "Participation of Children and Adolescents in Live Crisis Drills and Exercises," *Pediatrics* 146, no. 3 (2020), e2020015503, https://doi.org/10.1542/peds.2020-015503.

3. Laura S. Clarke, Dusty C. Embury, Ruth E. Jones, and Nina Yssel, "Supporting Students with Disabilities during School Crises: A Teacher's Guide," *Teaching Exceptional Children* 46, no. 6 (2014): 169–178, https://doi.org/10.1177/0040059914534616.

4. Clarke et al., "Supporting Students with Disabilities during School Crises"; Dusty Columbia Embury, Laura S. Clarke, and Kimberly Weber, "Keeping Our Students Safe during Crisis," *Physical Disabilities: Education and Related Services* 38, no. 1 (2019): 1–9, doi: 10.14434/pders.v38i1.27970, https://doi.org/10.14434/pders.v38i1.27970.

5. Stephen E. Brock, Amanda B. Nickerson, M.elissaA. Reeves, Christina Conolly, Shane R. Jimerson, Rosario C. Pesce, and Brian Lazzaro, *School Crisis Prevention and Intervention: The PREPaRE Model*, 2nd ed. (National Association of School Psychologists, 2016); see also Schonfeld et al., "Participation of Children and Adolescents in Live Crisis Drills.".

6. National Association of School Psychologists, "Mitigating Negative Psychological Effects of School Lockdown: Brief Guidance for

Schools" (2018), https://www.nasponline.org/resources-and-publications
/resources-and-podcasts/school-climate-safety-and-crisis/systems-level
-prevention/mitigating-psychological-effects-of-lockdowns.

7. US Department of Homeland Security, "Homeland Security Exercise
and Evaluation Program (HSEEP)" (2020), https://www.fema.gov/sites
/default/files/2020-04/Homeland-Security-Exercise-and-Evaluation
-Program-Doctrine-2020-Revision-2-2-25.pdf.

8. Partner Alliance for Safer Schools, "Safety and Security Guidelines
for K–12 Schools" (2020), https://passk12.org/guidelines-resources
/pass-school-security'-guidelines; Schonfeld et al., "Participation of
Children and Adolescents in Live Crisis Drills and Exercises."

9. "I Love U Guys" Foundation, "The Standard Response Protocol
K–12"; US Department of Education, "Final Report of the U.S. Federal Commission on School Safety" (2018), https://www2.ed.gov
/documents/school-safety/school-safety-report.pdf.

10. Schonfeld et al., "Participation of Children and Adolescents in
Live Crisis Drills and Exercises."

11. "I Love U Guys" Foundation, "The Standard Response Protocol
K–12"; National Association of School Psychologists, National Association of School Resource Officers, and Safe and Sound Schools, *Best Practice Considerations for Armed Assailant Drills in Schools*; National Child
Traumatic Stress Network, "Creating School Active Shooter/Intruder
Drills," brief (2018), https://www.nctsn.org/sites/default/files/resources
/fact-sheet/creating_school_active_shooter_intruder_drills.pdf.

12. Kristine M. Gebbie, Joan Valas, Jacqueline A. Merrill, and Stephen
S. Morse, "Role of Exercises and Drills in the Evaluation of Public
Health in Emergency Response," *Prehospital and Disaster Medicine* 21,
no. 3 (2006): 173–182, https://doi.org/10.1017/S1049023X00003642.

13. National Association of School Psychologists, National Association
of School Resource Officers, and Safe and Sound Schools, *Best Practice
Considerations for Armed Assailant Drills in Schools*; Safe and Sound
Schools, "The Toolkits: Assess, Act, & Audit," n.d., https://www.safe
andsoundschools.org/resources/the-toolkits-assess-act-and-audit.

14. US Department of Education Emergency Response and Crisis
Management Technical Assistance Center, "Integrating Students with
Special Needs and Disabilities into Emergency Response and Crisis

Management Planning," *ERCM Express* 2, no. 1 (2006). https://rems .ed.gov/docs/disability_newsletterv2I1.pdf.

15. Clarke et al., "Supporting Students with Disabilities during School Crises"; Columbia Embury, Clarke, and Weber, "Keeping Our Students Safe during Crisis."

16. Terri A. Erbacher and Scott Poland, "School Psychologists Must Be Involved in Planning and Conducting Active Shooter Drills," *NASP Communique* 48, no. 1 (September 2019): 10–13. https://static1.squarespace.com /static/5d63fedcb8c88e00011779a1/t/5d66b7892d18f0000121bda5 /1567012749149/School+Psychologists+Must+Be+Involved+in+Planning +and+Conducting+Active+Shooter+Drills+PDF.pdf; National Association of School Psychologists, "Mitigating Negative Psychological Effects of School Lockdown"; Schonfeld et al., "Participation of Children and Adolescents in Live Crisis Drills and Exercises."

17. Erbacher and Poland, "School Psychologists Must Be Involved in Planning and Conducting Active Shooter Drills."

18. Brock et al., *School Crisis Prevention and Intervention*"; "I Love U Guys" Foundation, "The Standard Response Protocol K–12,"

19. Jerry Nathan Moore, "Senate Bill 75: Active Shooter Intruder Response Training Perceptions of Building Leaders andTeachers from Southwest Missouri High Schools," PhD diss., Lindenwood University, 2015; Marizen Ramirez, Katrina Kubicek, Corinne Peek-Asa, and Marleen Wong, "Accountability and Assessment of Emergency Drill Performance at Schools," *Family & Community Health* 32, no. 2 (2009): 105–114, https://doi.org/10.1097/FCH.0b013e3181994662.

20. Karlene Tipler, Ruth Tarrant, Keith Tuffin, and David Johnston, "Learning from Experience: Emergency Response in Schools," *Natural Hazards* 90, no. 3 (2018): 1237–1257, https://doi.org/10.1007/s11069 -017-3094-x.

21. Korrie Allen, Edward Lorek, and Nita Mensia-Joseph, "Conducting a School-Based Mock Drill: Lessons Learned from One Community," *Biosecurity and Bioterrorism: Biodefense Strategy, Practice, and Science* 6, no. 2 (2008), 191–201, https://doi.org/10.1089/bsp.2007.0065.

22. Riswan Septriayadi Sianturi, Adjie Pamungkas, Ita Elysiyah, Arna Ferrajuanie, Retno Indro Putri, and Muhammad Yusuf, "Investigating the Response of Students with Disabilities to Earthquakes: Preliminary

Results," *IOP Conference Series: Earth and Environmental Science* 562 (2020): 012010, https://doi.org/10.1088/1755-1315/562/1/012010.

23. Amanda B. Nickerson, Pauline M. Pagliocca, and Samantha Palladino, "Research and Evaluation Needs for Crisis Intervention," in *Best Practices in Crisis Prevention and Intervention in the Schools,* 2nd ed., ed. Stephen E. Brock and Shane R. Jimerson (National Association of School Psychologists, 2012), 701–730.

24. Jaclyn Schildkraut, Amanda B. Nickerson, and Thomas Ristoff, "Locks, Lights, Out of Sight: Assessing Students' Perceptions of Emergency Preparedness across Multiple Lockdown Drills," *Journal of School Violence* 19, no. 1 (2020), 93–106, https://doi.org/10.1080/15388220 .2019.1703720.

CHAPTER 9

1. David L. Altheide, "The Columbine Shootings and the Discourse of Fear," *American Behavioral Scientist* 52, no. 10 (2009): 1354–1370, https:// doi.org/10.1177/0002764209332552; Randy Borum, Dewey G. Cornell, William Modzeleski, and Shane R. Jimerson, "What Can Be Done about School Shootings? A Review of the Evidence," *Educational Researcher* 39, no. 1 (2010): 27–37, https://doi.org/10.3102/0013189X09357620.

2. Thomas A. Birkland and Regina G. Lawrence, "Media Framing and Policy Change after Columbine," *American Behavioral Scientist* 52, no. 10 (2009): 1405–1425, https://doi.org/10.1177/0002764209332555; M. Franci Crepeau-Hobson, MaryLynne Filaccio, and Linda Gottfried, "Violence Prevention after Columbine: A Survey of High School Mental Health Professionals," *Children and Schools* 27, no. 3 (2005): 157–165, https://doi.org/10.1093/cs/27.3.157; Aaron Kupchik, John J. Brent, and Thomas J. Mowen, "The Aftermath of Newtown: More of the Same," *British Journal of Criminology* 55, no. 6 (2015): 1115–1130, https://doi.org/10.1093/bjc/azv049.

3. Sasha Abramsky, "The School-security Industry Is Cashing in Big on Public Fears of Mass Shootings," *Nation,* August 9, 2016, https://www .thenation.com/article/archive/the-school-security-industry-is-cashing -in-big-on-public-fears-of-mass-shootings; Jim Dearing, "School Security Systems Industry—US Market Overview," IHS Markit, February 26, 2018, https://omdia.tech.informa.com/OM002098/School-security-systems -industry---US-market-overview; Adrian Ma, "Anxiety over Shootings

Bolsters $2.7 Billion School Security Industry," Marketplace, May 8, 2018, https://www.marketplace.org/2018/05/08/anxiety-over-shootings -bolsters-27-billion-school-security-industry.

4. Ronnie Casella, "The False Allure of Security Technologies," *Social Justice* 30, no. 3 (2003): 82–93, https://www.jstor.org/stable/29768210.

5. Jennifer Hesterman, *Soft Target Hardening: Protecting People from Attack* (CRC Press, 2015).

6. Lynn A. Addington, "Cops and Cameras: Public School Security as a Policy Response to Columbine," *American Behavioral Scientist* 52, no. 10 (2009): 1426–1446, https://doi.org/10.1177/0002764209332556; Tyson Lewis, "The Surveillance Economy of Post-Columbine Schools," *Review of Education, Pedagogy, and Cultural Studies* 25, no. 4 (2003): 335–355, https://doi.org/10.1080/10714410390251101.

7. Ke Wang, Yongqiu Chen, Jizhi Zhang, and Barbara A. Oudekerk, "Indicators of School Crime and Safety: 2019" (National Center for Education Statistics, 2020), https://nces.ed.gov/pubs2020/2020063.pdf.

8. Brad Spicer, "11 Components of a Secure School Front Entrance," *Campus Safety Magazine*, October 23, 2013, https://www.campus safetymagazine.com/safety/11-components-of-a-secure-school -front-entrance.

9. Rachel Armitage, "Crime Prevention through Environmental Design," in *Environmental Criminology and Crime Analysis*, 2nd ed., ed. Richard Wortley and Michael Townsley (Routledge, 2017), 259–285; Paul Cozens, "Crime Prevention through Environmental Design," in *Environmental Criminology and Crime Analysis*, ed. Richard Wortley and Lorraine Mazerolle (Routledge, 2011), 153–177; C. Ray Jeffery, *Crime Prevention through Environmental Design* (Sage, 1971); Oscar Newman, *Defensible Space: Crime Prevention through Urban Design* (Macmillan, 1972); Oscar Newman, *Defensible Space: People and Design in the Violent City* (Architectural Press, 1973).

10. Spencer C. Weiler, and Martha Cray, "Police at School: A Brief History and Current Status of School Resource Officers," *Clearing House: A Journal of Educational Strategies, Issues and Ideas* 84, no. 4 (2011): 160–163, https://doi.org/10.1080/00098655.2011.564986.

11. Jaana Juvonen, "School Violence: Prevalence, Fears, and Prevention" (RAND Corp., 2001), https://www.rand.org/content/dam/rand /pubs/issue_papers/2006/IP219.pdf.

12. Marieke Brock, Norma Kriger, and Ramón Miró, "School Safety Policies and Programs Administered by the U.S. Federal Government: 1990–2016" (Office of Justice Programs, 2018), https://www.ojp.gov /pdffiles1/nij/grants/251517.pdf; Chelsea Connery, "The Prevalence and the Price of Police in Schools," policy brief (UCONN Center for Education Policy Analysis, 2020), https://cepa.uconn.edu/wp -content/uploads/sites/399/2020/10/Issue-Brief-CEPA_C-Connery .pdf.

13. US Department of Justice, Office of Community Policing Services, "About the COPS Office" (n.d.), https://cops.usdoj.gov/aboutcops.

14. Cheryl Lero Jonson, Alexander L. Burton, Francis T. Cullen, Justin T. Pickett, and Velmer S. Burton, "An Apple in One Hand, a Gun in the Other: Public Support for Arming our Nation's Schools," *Criminology & Public Policy* (2021), https://doi.org/10.1111/1745-9133.12538.

15. Tess Owen, "Exclusive: How Parkland Created a Rush to Arm Teachers and School Staff across the Country," *Vice*, January 9, 2019, https://www.vice.com/en/article/439z7q/exclusive-how-parkland -created-a-rush-to-arm-teachers-and-school-staff-across-the-country; RAND Corp., "The Effects of Laws Allowing Armed Staff in K–12 Schools" (April 2020), https://www.rand.org/research/gun-policy/anal ysis/laws-allowing-armed-staff-in-K12-schools.html.

16. Edward W. Hill, "The Cost of Arming Schools: The Price of Stopping a Bad Guy with a Gun," faculty paper, Cleveland State University, 2013, https://engagedscholarship.csuohio.edu/urban_facpub/678.

17. US Department of Justice, Office of Community Policing Services, "Fact Sheet: 2017 COPS Hiring Program" (2017), https://cops.usdoj .gov/pdf/2017AwardDocs/chp/Post_Award_Fact_Sheet.pdf.

18. Todd A. DeMitchell and Christine C. Rath, "Armed and Dangerous—Teachers? A Policy Response to Security in our Public Schools," *Brigham Young University Education and Law Journal* 2019, no. 1 (2019): 63–93, https://digitalcommons.law.byu.edu/elj/vol2019/iss1/4; United Educators, "Increased Risks and Costs of Arming Educators," EduRisk Solutions: Insights, June 2020. https://www.edurisksolutions .org/blogs/?Id=3763.

19. Judith Lohman and Alan Shephard, "School Security Technologies" (Connecticut General Assembly, Office of Legislative Research, 2006), https://www.cga.ct.gov/2006/rpt/2006-R-0668.htm.

20. Ronet Bachman, Antonia Randolph, and Bethany L. Brown, "Predicting Perceptions of Fear at School and Going to and from School for African American and White Students: The Effect of School Security Measures," *Youth & Society* 43, no. 2 (2011): 705–726, https://doi.org/10.1177/0044118X10366674.

21. Suzanne E. Perumean-Chaney and Lindsay M. Sutton, "Students and Perceived School Safety: School Security Measures," *American Journal of Criminal Justice* 38, no. 4 (2013): 570–588, https://doi.org/10.1007/s12103-012-9182-2.

22. Christen Pentek and Marla E. Eisenberg, "School Resource Officers, Safety, and Discipline: Perceptions and Experiences across Racial/ethnic Groups in Minnesota Secondary Schools," *Children and Youth Services Review* 88 (2018): 141–148, https://doi.org/10.1016/j.childyouth.2018.03.008; Madina Toure, "Use of Metal Detectors in New York City Schools Under Scrutiny amid Parkland Shooting," *Observer*, March 9, 2018, http://observer.com/2018/03/metal-detectors-nyc-public-schools; Erica O. Turner and Abigail J. Beneke, "'Softening' School Resource Officers: The Extension of Police Presence in Schools in an Era of Black Lives Matter, School Shootings, and Rising Inequality," *Race Ethnicity and Education* 23, no. 2 (2020): 221–240, https://doi.org/10.1080/13613324.2019.1679753.

23. WNYC, "Metal Detectors in New York City High Schools" (n.d.), https://project.wnyc.org/metal-detectors.

24. National Association of School Resource Officers, "NASRO Opposes Arming Teachers," press release, February 22, 2018. https://www.nasro.org/news/2018/02/22/news-releases/nasro-opposes-arming-teachers; Sonali Rajan and Charles C. Branas, "Arming Schoolteachers: What Do We Know? Where Do We Go from Here?," *American Journal of Public Health* 108, no. 7 (2018): 860–862, https://ajph.aphapublications.org/doi/10.2105/AJPH.2018.304464; Danielle Weatherby, "Opening the Snake Pit: Arming Teachers in the War against School Violence and the Government-created Risk Doctrine," *Connecticut Law Review* 48, 1 (2015): 119–176, https://opencommons.uconn.edu/cgi/viewcontent.cgi?article=1300&context=law_review.

25. WNYC, "Metal Detectors in New York City High Schools."

26. Zach Winn, "NYC School Safety Agents Find 328 Weapons in 3 Months," *Campus Safety Magazine*, October 4, 2017, https://www

.campussafetymagazine.com/safety/nyc-school-safety-agents-find-328-weapons-in-3-months.

27. White House, "Presidential Policy Directive/PPD-8: National Preparedness," March 30, 2011, https://www.hsdl.org/?view&did=7423.

28. US Department of Education, Office of Elementary and Secondary Education, Office of Safe and Healthy Students, "Guide for Developing High-Quality School Emergency Operations Plans" (2013), https://www.dhs.gov/sites/default/files/publications/REMS%20K-12%20Guide%20508_0.pdf.

29. US Department of Education, Office of Elementary and Secondary Education, Office of Safe and Supportive Schools, "The Role of Districts in Developing High-quality School Emergency Operations Plans" (2019), https://rems.ed.gov/docs/District_Guide_508C.pdf.

30. Stephen E. Brock, Amanda B. Nickerson, Melissa A. Reeves, Christina Conolly, Shane R. Jimerson, Rosasrio C. Pesce, and Brian Lazzaro, *School Crisis Prevention and Intervention: The PREPaRE Model,* 2nd ed. (National Association of School Psychologists, 2016).

31. US Department of Homeland Security, Federal Emergency Management Agency, "National Incident Management System" (December 2008), http://www.fema.gov/pdf/emergency/nims/NIMS_core.pdf.

32. Amanda B. Nickerson, Stephen E. Brock, and Melissa A. Reeves, "School Crisis Teams within an Incident Command System," *California School* 11 (2006): 51–60, https://doi.org/10.1007/BF03341116.

33. Katherine C. Cowan, Kelly Vaillancourt, Eric Rossen, and Kelly Pollitt, "A Framework for Safe and Successful Schools" (National Association of School Psychologists, 2013), https://www.nasponline.org/Documents/Research%20and%20Policy/Advocacy%20Resources/Framework_for_Safe_and_Successful_School_Environments.pdf.

34. Tod Schneider, Hill Walker, and Jeffrey Sprague, *Safe School Design: A Handbook for Educational Leaders Applying the Principles of Crime Prevention through Environmental Design* (ERIC Clearinghouse on Educational Management, 2000), https://eric.ed.gov/?id=ED449541; Jeffrey R. Sprague and Hill M. Walker, *Safe and Healthy Schools: Practical Prevention Strategies* (Guilford Press, 2005).

35. Daniel Lamoreaux and Michael L. Sulkowski, "An Alternative to Fortified Schools: Using Crime Prevention through Environmental Design (CPTED) to Balance Student Safety and Psychological

Well-Being," *Psychology in the Schools* 57, no. 1 (2020): 152–165, https://doi.org/10.1002/pits.22301; Sarah Lindstrom Johnson, Tracy Evian Waasdorp, Anne Henry Cash, Katrina J. Debnam, Adam J. Milam, and Catherine P. Bradshaw, "Assessing the Association between observed School Disorganization and School Violence: Implications for School Climate Interventions," *Psychology of Violence* 7(2 (2017): 181–191, https://doi.org/10.1037/vio0000045.

36. Amanda B. Nickerson and Dewey Cornell, "Crisis Prevention, Response, and Recovery," in *School Safety and Violence Prevention: Science, Practice, and Policy Driving Change*, ed. Matthew J. Mayer and Shane R. Jimerson (American Psychological Association, 2019), 223–246.

CHAPTER 10

1. Joe Heim and Valerie Strauss, "In Capitol Riot, Some Hill Staffers Recall Their School-Shooting Drills," *Philadelphia Inquirer*, January 14, 2021, https://www.inquirer.com/politics/nation/capitol-attack-insurrection-hill-staffers-remembered-school-shooting-drills-20210115.html.

2. Children's Defense Fund, "School Shootings Spark Everyday Worries: Children and Parents Call for Safe Schools and Neighborhoods (2018), https://www.childrensdefense.org/wp-content/uploads/2018/09/YouGov-SafeSchools-Final-Sep-18-2018.pdf; Nikki Graf, "A Majority of U.S. Teens Fear a Shooting Could Happen at their School, and Most Parents Share their Concern" (Pew Research Center, 2018), https://www.pewresearch.org/fact-tank/2018/04/18/a-majority-of-u-s-teens-fear-a-shooting-could-happen-at-their-school-and-most-parents-share-their-concern.

3. Jim Norman, "Four in 10 Teachers Say Their School Is Not Well Prepared," Gallup, March 22, 2018, https://news.gallup.com/poll/230366/four-teachers-say-school-not-protected.aspx.

4. Based on authors' data, available on request.

5. Bruria Adini, Avishay Goldberg, Robert Cohen, Daniel Laor, and Yaron Bar-Dayan, "Evidence-Based Support for the All-Hazards Approach to Emergency Preparedness," *Israel Journal of Health Policy Research* 1 (2012): 40, https://doi.org/10.1186/2045-4015-1-40; Readiness and Emergency Management for Schools Technical Assistance Center, "Using an All-Hazards Approach When Planning for Emergency Incidents" (n.d.), https://rems.ed.gov/Resource_Plan_Basic_All_Hazard.aspx.

6. Kara M. Stephens, "All-Hazards Preparedness Guide" (Centers for Disease Control and Prevention, 2013), https://www.cdc.gov/cpr/documents/AHPG_FINAL_March_2013.pdf.

7. Ready.gov, "Disasters and Emergencies" (2021), https://www.ready.gov/be-informed.

8. Department of Homeland Security, "National Preparedness System," 2011, https://www.fema.gov/pdf/prepared/nps_description.pdf.

9. Readiness and Emergency Management for Schools Technical Assistance Center, "Threat- and Hazard-Specific Annexes" (n.d.), https://rems.ed.gov/K12ThreatAndHSAnnex.aspx; see also Readiness and Emergency Management for Schools Technical Assistance Center. "Using an All-Hazards Approach When Planning for Emergency Incidents."

10. National Association of School Psychologists, National Association of School Resource Officers, and Safe and Sound Schools, *Best Practice Considerations for Armed Assailant Drills in Schools* (2021), https://www.nasponline.org/Documents/Research%20and%20Policy/Advocacy%20Resources/Armed-Assailant-Guide-FINAL.pdf.

11. James M. Kendra and Tricia Wachtendorf, "Creativity in Emergency Response to the World Trade Center Disaster," in *Beyond September 11th: An Account of Post-Disaster Research* (Natural Hazards Research and Information Center, 2003), https://hazards.colorado.edu/archive/publications/sp/sp39/BeyondSeptember11th.pdf#page=132.

12. Joachim Ahrens and Patrick M. Rudolph, "The Importance of Governance in Risk Reduction and Disaster Management," *Journal of Contingencies and Crisis Management* 14, no. 4 (2006): 207–220, https://doi.org/10.1111/j.1468-5973.2006.00497.x.

13. Kristin M. Holland, Jeffrey E. Hall, Jing Wang, Elizabeth M. Gaylor, Linda L. Johnson, Daniel Shelby, and Thomas R. Simon, and School-Associated Violent Deaths Study Group, "Characteristics of School-Associated Youth Homicides—United States, 1994–2018," *Morbidity and Mortality Weekly Report*, 68, no. 3 (2019): 53–60, https://doi.org/10.15585/mmwr.mm6803a1.

14. National Association of School Psychologists, "Preventing Youth Suicide: Brief Facts and Tips" (2015), https://www.nasponline.org/resources-and-publications/resources-and-podcasts/school-climate-safety-and-crisis/mental-health-resources/preventing-youth-suicide.

15. Centers for Disease Control and Prevention, National Center for Health Statistics, "Wide-ranging OnLine Data for Epidemiologic Research (WONDER): Underlying Cause of Death 1999–2019," data set (2020), http://wonder.cdc.gov/ucd-icd10.html.

16. National Center for Education Statistics, "Student Reports of Bullying: Results from the 2017 School Crime Supplement to the National Crime Victimization Survey" (2019), https://nces.ed.gov/pubs2019/2019054.pdf.

17. National Association of School Psychologists, "Threat Assessment at School: Brief Facts and Tips" (2015), https://www.nasponline.org/resources-and-publications/resources-and-podcasts/school-climate-safety-and-crisis/systems-level-prevention/threat-assessment-at-school.

18. Bryan Vossekuil, Robert A. Fein, Marisa Reddy, Randy Borum, and William Modzeleski, "The Final Report and Findings of the Safe School Initiative: Implications for the Prevention of School Attacks in the United States" (US Secret Service and US Department of Education, 2004), https://www2.ed.gov/admins/lead/safety/preventingattacksreport.pdf.

19. Keith J. Zullig, "Active Shooter Drills: A Closer Look at Next Steps," *Journal of Adolescent Health* 67, no. 4 (2020): 465–466, https://doi.org/10.1016/j.jadohealth.2020.07.028.

20. US Department of Homeland Security, Federal Emergency Management Agency, US Fire Administration, "School Building Fires (2009–2011)" (National Fire Data Center, 2014), https://www.usfa.fema.gov/downloads/pdf/statistics/v14i14.pdf.

ESSENTIAL READINGS

The reports and research studies highlighted below provide an important starting point for those wishing to learn more about lockdown drills and their impacts. These resources can be used by school policymakers and administrators as they develop and implement their own all-hazards emergency response plans, of which lockdowns are one of several critical components. They also may be useful to educators and parents seeking to understand the best way to conduct these practices to minimize potential harm to participants and to configure them as valuable learning experiences that can empower students to take an active, even proactive, role in their personal safety.

GUIDANCE AND BEST PRACTICE DOCUMENTATION

National Association of School Psychologists. "Conducting Crisis Exercises and Drills: Guidelines for Schools," 2013. https://www.nasponline .org/resources-and-publications/resources-and-podcasts/school-climate -safety-and-crisis/systems-level-prevention/conducting-crisis-exercises -and-drills.

National Association of School Psychologists, National Association of School Resource Officers, and Safe and Sound Schools, *Best Practice Considerations for Armed Assailant Drills in Schools*, 2021. https://www

.nasponline.org/Documents/Research%20and%20Policy/Advocacy%20
Resources/Armed-Assailant-Guide-FINAL.pdf.

National Association of School Psychologists. *Mitigating Negative Psychological Effects of School Lockdown: Brief Guidance for Schools*, 2018.
https://www.nasponline.org/resources-and-publications/resources-and
-podcasts/school-climate-safety-and-crisis/systems-level-prevention
/mitigating-psychological-effects-of-lockdowns.

US Department of Education, Office of Elementary and Secondary
Education, Office of Safe and Healthy Students. *Guide for Developing High-Quality School Emergency Operations Plans*, 2013. https://
mk0edsource0y23p672y.kinstacdn.com/wp-content/uploads/old
/REMS_K-12_Guide_508.pdf.

US Department of Education, Office of Elementary and Secondary
Education, Office of Safe and Healthy Students. *The Role of Districts in Developing High-Quality School Emergency Operations Plans*, 2019.
https://rems.ed.gov/docs/District_Guide_508C.pdf.

US Department of Education, Emergency Response and Crisis Management Technical Assistance Center. "Integrating Students with Special
Needs and Disabilities into Emergency Response and Crisis Management Planning." *ERCM Express*, 2, no. 1 (2006). https://rems.ed.gov
/docs/disability_newsletterv2I1.pdf.

US Department of Homeland Security. *Active Shooter: How to Respond*,
2008. https://www.dhs.gov/xlibrary/assets/active_shooter_booklet.pdf.

US Department of Homeland Security, Federal Emergency Management Agency. "Be Prepared for an Active Shooter," 2018. https://www
.fema.gov/media-library-data/1523561958719-f1eff6bc841d56b7873e
018f73a4e024/ActiveShooter_508.pdf.

RESEARCH STUDIES

Clark, Kevin R., Suzieann M. Bass, and Sonja K. Boiteaux. "Survey
of Educators' Preparedness to Respond to Active Shooter Incidents."
Radiologic Technology 90, no. (2019): 541–551. https://pubmed.ncbi
.nlm.nih.gov/31270255/.

Dickson, Misty Jo, and Kristina K. Vargo. "Training Kindergarten
Students: Lockdown Drill Procedures using Behavioral Skills Training.

Journal of Applied Behavioral Analysis 50, no. 2 (2017): 407–412. https://doi.org/10.1002/jaba.369.

Jonson, Cheryl Lero, Melissa M. Moon, and Brooke Miller Gialopsos. "Are Students Scared or Prepared? Psychological Impacts of a Multi-Option Active Assailant Protocol Compared to Other Crisis/Emergency Preparedness Practices." *Victims & Offenders* 15, no. 5 (2020): 639–662. https://doi.org/10.1080/15564886.2020.1753871.

Jonson, Cheryl Lero, Melissa M., Moon, and Joseph A. Hendry. "One Size Does Not Fit All: Traditional Lockdown versus Multioption Responses to School Shootings." *Journal of School Violence,* 19, no. 2 (2020): 154–166. https://doi.org/10.1080/15388220.2018.1553719.

Moore-Petinak, N'dea, Marika Waselewski, Blaire Alma Patterson, and Tammy Chang. "Active Shooter Drills in the United States: A National Study of Youth Experiences and Perceptions." *Journal of Adolescent Health* 67, no. 4 (2020): 509–513. https://doi.org/10.1016/j.jadohealth.2020.06.015.

Nickerson, Amanda B., and Jaclyn Schildkraut. "State Anxiety prior to and after Participating in Lockdown Drills among Students in a rural High School." *School Psychology Review,* 2021. https://doi.org/10.1080/2372966X.2021.1875790.

Perkins, Jane C. "Preparing Teachers for School Tragedy: Reading, Writing, and Lockdown." *Journal of Higher Education Theory and Practice* 18, no. 1 (2018): 70–81. http://m.www.na-businesspress.com/JHETP/JHETP18-1/PerkinsJC_18_1.pdf.

Schildkraut, Jaclyn, and Amanda B. Nickerson. "Ready to Respond: Effects of Lockdown Drills and Training on School Emergency Preparedness." *Victims & Offenders* 15, no. 5 (2020): 619–638. https://doi.org/10.1080/15564886.2020.1749199.

Schildkraut, Jaclyn, Amanda B. Nickerson, and Kirsten R. Klingaman. "Reading, Writing, Responding: Educators' Perceptions of Safety, Preparedness, and Lockdown drills." *Educational Policy, 2021.* https://doi.org/10.1177/08959048211015617.

Schildkraut, Jaclyn, Amanda B. Nickerson, and Thomas Ristoff. "Locks, Lights, Out of Sight: Assessing Students' Perceptions of Emergency Preparedness across Multiple Lockdown Drills." *Journal of School*

Violence 19, no. 1 (2020): 93–106. https://doi.org/10.1080/15388220.2019.1703720.

Schonfeld, David J., Marlene Melzer-Lange, Andrew N. Hashikawa, Peter A. Gorski, and American Academy of Pediatrics Council on Children and Disasters, Council on Injury, Violence, and Poison Prevention, Council on School Health. "Participation of Children and Adolescents in live Crisis Drills and Exercises." *Pediatrics* 146, no. 3 (2020): e2020015503. https://doi.org/10.1542/peds.2020-015503.

Zhe, Elizabeth J., and Amanda B. Nickerson. "Effects of an Intruder Crisis Drill on Children's Knowledge, Anxiety, and Perceptions of School Safety." *School Psychology Review* 36, no. 3 (2007): 501–508. https://doi.org/10.1080/02796015.2007.12087936.

INDEX